BOOT★CAMP
DIGITAL

The **Ultimate** Guide™

Digital Marketing
That Works
ACTUALLY

krista neher

For general information on our other products and for services or technical support please see www.bootcampdigital.com or Contact Customer Care at 513-223-3878.

ISBN-13: 978-0-9830286-4-2

Printed in the United States of America

First Edition

Thank you to the team that helped bring this book to life: Allison, Joe, Lirie and Melissa. This was truly a team effort.

#ThinkImpact

How to Use This Book

This book is designed to give you an overview of digital marketing strategies, tools and tactics but also empower you with a solid understanding for implementation. Whether you are a digital marketer, a brand manager, an agency pro, an entrepreneur, a business leader or a professional wanting to grow your knowledge, this book will put you on the path to success.

To maximize your value from the book, you'll see icons and specific call-outs to draw your attention to elements that are important to your success. You'll see these throughout the book.

Tools
You'll get recommendations on specific tools or resources that you can use to implement.

Power Tip
This is a high-impact tip that can really impact your success and results. These are easy to implement.

Remember
This is an important point that you will want to keep in mind going forward.

Big Idea
This is an idea that is central to the topic and should get you thinking about how to drive your results.

Action Item
We'll draw your attention to things that you should do immediately. (You can also save these to do later)

Example
Examples that bring the concept to life are highlighted. This helps in implementation.

Table of Contents

Introduction

Digital marketing has been around for over 20 years, but we are currently at a tipping point, with over 50% of marketing budgets going towards digital.

The true power of digital marketing isn't in the amount of spending it accounts for – it's in the power that digital marketing brings to entrepreneurs, small business owners, and Fortune 100 companies. It's no longer about the biggest spender winning. It's about the smartest marketer.

Digital marketing has the following benefits for businesses of any size or in any industry:

- Budget – Digital marketing works on almost any budget.
- Speed – Campaigns can be executed quickly.
- Results – Results are immediately available to know what works.
- Flexibility – If something isn't working you can adapt quickly.
- Optimization – Real-time data lets you improve results.

This book is broken down into three main sections. The first is **digital marketing strategy**, which answers the question of WHY you are using digital marketing and HOW it can grow your business.

Part 2 of this book is dedicated to a deep dive on **digital marketing tactics**. Once you understand your goal, strategy, and objectives you will be able to choose the digital marketing tools that are most likely to drive your business results.

The third section of the book covers **measurement, priority setting and action planning**. Here you will learn how to know if your efforts are working and how to interpret the results. This section also covers priority setting so you can determine where you can have the biggest impact and focus on what will drive your business forward.

There are many things within digital marketing that you **could do** – the question is what you **should do.** There are two frameworks to help you understand this.

Isn't Digital Marketing Always Changing?

I'm often asked how I can write a book on digital marketing since it changes so quickly. While many of the tactics and details are rapidly evolving, digital marketing strategies, channels, and tools are actually fairly stable over time.

I started in social media marketing in 2007 and, even now, the major social networks work roughly the same way they always did, and the keys to success are alarmingly similar. The tactics I used to gain a Twitter following for my business in 2007 are the same things that work now. Sure there are new features and tricks, but by and large, the approach is the same.

While digital marketing does change and evolve, the change isn't as rapid as some alarmists would have you believe. Businesses that focus on tricks or hacks (how to get a million Instagram followers overnight!!!!) will probably find they need to adapt quickly as these gimmicks are usually short-lived in their effectiveness.

Remember:
Businesses focusing on a solid strategy will find that the world of digital marketing doesn't change as quickly, and they can focus their efforts on refining and improving the strategies that work.

Focus on Foundations

I work with many different businesses – from billion-dollar global fortune 100 companies to small mom-and-pop shops with little marketing spending, and they all have the same big opportunity.

Focus on Foundations.

It's easy to get distracted by the new and upcoming digital marketing trends, but the reality is that most businesses can drive bigger impact by more successfully implementing the foundations.

When it comes to growing a business with digital marketing, success comes from mastering the core areas of digital marketing that we know matter – Social Media, Advertising, and Websites. Not from new tools or technologies.

The most common questions I get in my Digital Marketing Boot Camps are about new tools or trends. The reality is that most businesses aren't executing the foundations with excellence.

Their website is slow. They don't have great content on Facebook. Their ads aren't optimized.

This book focuses on the foundations of a solid digital marketing strategy that actually works. Simply put, they get results that grow your business.

Don't be distracted. Focus on doing the things that work better. They will drive more ROI vs. shiny new objects.

PART 1: DIGITAL MARKETING STRATEGY

When it comes to digital marketing, many businesses dive in and get started with tactics right away – they get on Facebook, they start Google Ads, they initiate the new website design.

Starting with tactics instead of strategy creates two problems. The first is that the execution is often not as effective as it could be because there isn't a clear idea of WHY they are doing what they are.

 I recently worked with a billion-dollar multinational company and in a coaching session with the CEO he asked about their website. Was their website any good? My first question was, what was the website supposed to do? What was the marketing strategy and digital marketing strategy for the website?

Sure, the site looked nice, but there was no real focus for a consumer. The marketing strategy was clear: Drive word-of-mouth and trial of the product. The website, while beautiful, didn't do either of these things.

A clear strategy should be visible in every execution, and a more strategic execution built with the strategy in mind is more likely to deliver business value. It will also make executing easier as you will have a clear lens to judge your digital marketing efforts by assessing whether or not it's achieving your strategy.

The second challenge is that without a clear idea of the strategy, it's difficult, if not impossible to judge your success.

 The same business I mentioned above wanted to know if their site was working well. I could show him Google Analytics and give him no end of reports on the time on site, bounce rates, page visits, etc., but I first asked the question, what is the website supposed to do? What is the strategy for the website? Without knowing what the strategy was – what purpose did the website serve in the marketing strategy – it was difficult to measure the success. A million unique visitors, for example, don't matter if zero sign up to try the product.

While it may seem easier to start with tactics or execution, always start with strategy. This section will show you exactly how to create a solid digital marketing strategy that is the foundation for all of your digital marketing efforts.

Chapter 1: Steps to Building a Digital Marketing Plan

Whether you create a formal plan for a CMO or Board of Directors, or a simple plan for yourself, stepping back and building that plan is important to keep your efforts focused and on-track for delivering business value.

Often times businesses of all sizes start with the tactics – websites, chatbots, search ads – without a clear vision for the bigger picture. Whether you are initiating your digital marketing efforts or have been running digital marketing for some time, it is helpful to create or revise your plan to be sure that you're spending your time and resources as effectively as possible.

Big Idea:
Regardless of whether you're creating a new digital marketing plan or looking to get better results from an existing one, take the time to complete each of the steps in building a plan to add clarity and focus to your efforts.

Keep these steps in mind as you evaluate your processes and workflow, as well. Whether you are implementing yourself or using an agency, be sure you have regular reporting, measuring, and optimization built in to your execution.

Digital Marketing Plan: Overview

As you execute digital marketing or evaluate the effectiveness of any marketing – your website, email, Facebook page, ad campaign – you'll want to evaluate it against the lens of whether or not it is helping you achieve your plan.

There are eight steps to building and executing a strong digital marketing plan. These steps will all be covered in more detail throughout this book.

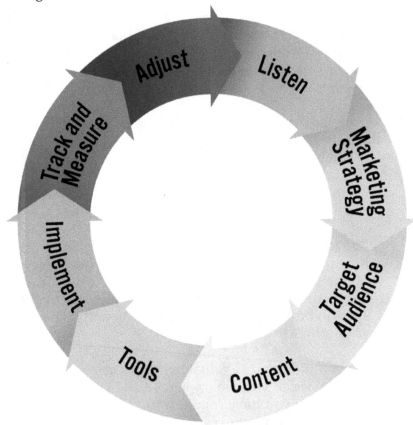

- **Listen** – Listening is the first and most important step – some say it is unexpectedly the most valuable step in this process! Take some time to look at your competitors, other industry players, and your target audience. The biggest challenges in growing your business with digital marketing is to have good ideas and execute them with excellence, and this step will help with both of these.

- **Marketing Strategy** – Clearly define your goal, strategy and objectives so that you have a clear idea of how your efforts will contribute to your bottom line. While this may seem obvious – grow sales, gain donations, increase registrations, etc. – clearly defining what *drives* your goal will add focus and effectiveness to your execution.

- **Target Audience** – The more clearly you define your target audience the better results you will get. Digital marketing allows us to use precision marketing to reach the exact right person at the exact right time with the exact right message. The challenge is knowing your audience specifically and intimately enough to execute this.

- **Content** – While content is ultimately a part of the execution of each channel, it's usually helpful to determine the content that your audience is interested in upfront. Crafting compelling content that breaks through digital clutter is key to stand out in a crowded marketplace.

- **Tools** – There are TONS of digital marketing channels and tools that you could use – websites, Facebook, email, CRM, etc. The key is choosing the right tools to meet your business objectives and focusing your efforts smartly.

- **Implement** – Implementing with excellence can make or break your success. Often with digital marketing the devil is in the details and maintaining excellence and using best practices is key.

- **Track and Measure** – For all the focus on digital marketing reporting and data, most of us still don't spend enough time looking at our results or using available data to inform our choices and improve our efforts over time.

- **Adjust** – Adaptability is the key to success and, as marketers, we need to change our mindset. When something is executed the real work is usually just beginning. Paying attention to performance and improving over time is key to growing your success in a changing digital ecosystem.

Action Planning:
The rest of this book will go through the steps above in more detail. To make the most out of this book, download your **Free Digital Marketing Plan Template at ThatActuallyWorksBooks.com/DM** to build your plan as you read this book.

Steps to Building a Digital Marketing Plan

> ➤ Do you have a business plan or strategy?
> ➤ Do you have a marketing plan or strategy?
> ➤ What do you want to achieve with digital marketing for your business?

_____

_____

_____

_____

_____

_____

_____

_____

What is the big thing you want to remember from this chapter?

_____

_____

Go to www.ThatActuallyWorks.com/DigitalMarketing for your free action planner and bonus resources.

Chapter 2: Listening and Assessing the Landscape

We often start by doing, but one of the best things about digital marketing is transparency – you can actually see what your competitors or other big brands are doing and learn from it.

 In a recent website project with a small business they were able to create an excellent website that improved sales over 100% by looking at what established players were doing and replicating their design elements. While your goal shouldn't be to copy your competitors, you can learn a lot by looking and listening.

 In working with a global fast food restaurant, we found that their content wasn't resonating. We looked at small businesses that were getting tons of engagement and learned from their strategies.

 A B2B business was struggling to find content for their website. We investigated top articles from industry news sites and articles on popular news sites like Buzzfeed. They refreshed their content strategy and saw a 500% increase in traffic.

The stage of listening is one of exploration and discovery. Have a pen and paper handy or a document ready to write down ideas, best practices, or tips that you discover along the way.

Big Idea:
Return back to the listening stage throughout building and executing your digital marketing plan. For example, as you consider growing your business on Instagram, go back and spend time looking on Instagram to generate new ideas and refresh on best practices.

What to Listen For

There are 5 things that you can listen for in digital marketing: your brand or company, your competitors, your industry or category, best-in class executors, and your target audience.

#1: Your Brand or Company
The first stage of listening is listening to and observing conversations about your brand and your company. What are people saying about your brand? What are the good and bad things being said? How do people feel about your company?

Listen to the conversations taking place on blogs, Twitter, Pinterest, discussion forums, websites, LinkedIn, Facebook, etc., to understand how you are perceived. This will help you understand where your opportunities lie. In addition, understanding what consumers are already saying about you will help you prepare responses for common questions or issues. It can help you anticipate areas that you should be prepared to address when you become active in social media.

#2: Your Competitors
Next, listen to what people are saying about your competitors and what your competitors are saying about themselves. What do

people say about your competitors in the social space? What are the pros and cons? How might this impact your business? Are there opportunities for you?

In addition to listening to how people feel about your competitors, it's helpful to identify the competitive social media landscape. What are your competitors doing on social media? Who are they targeting? What seems to work? What doesn't work? What can you learn from them? How can you approach this better than they are?

Power Tip:
Look up your key competitors across all social channels and try to gain insights on their strategy as well as the results of their efforts. You can often learn about their marketing and business strategy from what they post online. Indicators such as likes and engagements can also give you perspective as to how their content is actually performing.

#3: Your Industry or Category

After observing your competition, take your listening up a notch to the industry. What are consumers, potential consumers, or people in your target audience saying about your industry? What is the sentiment? Does this create opportunities? What conversations do they have around the industry? What are the passion points and pain points?

Developing an understanding of the conversations taking place around your industry will help you understand your space more broadly.

When I started in digital marketing working for a photography start-up, I listened on photography websites and discussion forums and used this to create a content calendar. In a short time, we had one of the top-rated photography blogs because we built content that people really wanted.

#4: Best in Class Executors

It can also be helpful to benchmark and keep a list of businesses similar to yours that are executing exceptionally well. These often won't be direct competitors, but maybe sites that execute strategies similar to yours.

For example, a small flower shop wanted to improve their ecommerce, so they looked at some small business ecommerce leaders and Shopify stores to solidify their execution. This gave them tons of new ideas like integrating reviews and ratings, how the cart should look, the images required to drive purchases, and even ideas about the types of photos they could include.

Power Tip:
Find and keep a list of competitors (or other businesses) who are doing well. For example, at Boot Camp Digital when we want to look at how to execute a subscription model we look at Netflix, Lynda.com, and Amazon. When we want to execute email excellence we have a few email campaigns we subscribe to that we can learn from.

#5: Your Target

The final stage of listening is to listen to and really get to understand your target audience. Find a handful of people that represent the audience you want to reach. What lingo and tone do they use? How do they interact with each other? What are the words that they naturally use to describe their feelings around your brand, competitors, or industry? What else do they talk about? What is on their mind? What are the unwritten rules of participation? Who is getting attention? Who are the influencers? How do they talk and what are they interested in?

Understanding your audience more deeply will pay dividends on every aspect of your digital marketing execution.

Where to Listen

There are a number of tools that you can use to listen online. One of the best things about digital marketing is the sheer amount of information that you have access to at your fingertips. As you start listening, here are some places and tools that you can use.

Google Search
Simply do a Google search and see what shows up. Google tries to show people the most relevant results based on what they're looking for, so this can give you insights into what Google thinks is relevant.

Explore the first page of search results but also look at other types of results like news, maps, videos, and images to see additional content that is relevant for your search term.

Use the related searches ("Searches related to..." at the bottom of the Google search results) to gain additional insights into the types of content and topics your audience searches for and is interested in.

Searches related to digital marketing training	
digital marketing training **free**	**best online** digital marketing **courses**
digital marketing **certificate**	**online** marketing **courses with certificates**
digital marketing **institute**	digital marketing **institute reviews**
digital marketing **certification**	digital marketing **course near me**

Power Tip:
Set up Google Alerts for your business and your competitors to be the first to know about related news. Go to alerts.google.com to set up your alert and get emailed when news or new results come up.

Google Trends
Google Trends (trends.google.com) allows you to see search data for specific categories, topics, or keywords. Trend data displays the trends over time and allows you to benchmark. Some studies have shown that search data can even be a proxy for market share, so seeing searches of your business relative to competitors can be insightful.

Google Keyword Tool
The Google Keyword Tool is available within Google Ads (ads.google.com). You need a Google Ad account to access it. This will show you search volume and competitiveness for search terms. This can be helpful to understand what people are looking for and the words and phrases they use.

Facebook
As the largest social network, Facebook is a great place to listen. The challenge on Facebook is that most personal posts and groups are private, so you can only listen to Pages and public conversations.

Power Tip:
A new feature in Facebook allows you to see all of the ads that your competitors are running. Simply go to their Page and click on Info and Ads on the left navigation and you can see all of their current ads.

Twitter
Twitter is still one of the top social networks and is heavily used by thought leaders and influencers. What makes Twitter a valuable place to listen is that most conversations are public. Twitter has

great search capabilities and you can even search by location to get more specific insights.

Pinterest
80% of the content on Pinterest is re-Pins – that means that someone shared something that they found interesting. On most other social networks, you find what brands want to post or the opinions people have. On Pinterest you can find what they share. It does tend to be overly female in users and the content is only visual, but you can get a lot of inspiration and insights.

Power Tip:
Once you search for a term on Pinterest you'll see categories below. Take note of the categories that Pinterest suggests for your search terms as these are the most common things that people search for and post about.

Instagram
Instagram is big and growing, and many people still keep their accounts public, so you can gain a lot of insights from searching here. Search for relevant hashtags or explore accounts and followers of people relevant for your business.

Power Tip:
The Instagram Explore page allows you to explore related content based on posts you've liked and people you follow. Be strategic about the posts and accounts you like, to discover other relevant content and people.

LinkedIn
LinkedIn is highly relevant for business or professional topics. Almost all content on LinkedIn is public, making it a great place for research and searching. LinkedIn now also has searchable hashtags which can make content easier to find. Also consider groups as a way to search beyond profiles, pages, and status updates.

YouTube
Video content is among the most popular content online, and YouTube is, by far, the most popular video network. Searches on YouTube will show a variety of content, and looking at popular content can also provide a good source of creative inspiration.

Discussion Forums
Discussion Forums are often heavily used by interested communities. There are discussion forums for moms, car enthusiasts, marketers, doctors, lawyers and more. Discussions are also now taking place in Facebook groups. Many of these are private, but you can always request to join. There are also broader discussion forums like Reddit that cover a wide range of topics. Look for forums used by your target audience or where your products are discussed.

Industry News Sites
Industry-specific news sites or associations can also be good sources of information as these groups typically have their finger on the pulse of the industry.

In my 15 years of digital marketing experience working with clients across various industries this stage has always been where I've generated the most insight for my clients. What is always surprising is that they could (and should) be doing this as a part of marketing and business on an ongoing basis, but most of us are so busy with daily tasks, that we don't step back often enough.

Action Planning:
Step back and spend some time looking and listening. Write down your key ideas, insights, and aha moments. Note businesses who are winning (and not winning) and learn as much as possible to better inform your efforts.

Big Idea:
Set a calendar appointment for yourself for a day (or a half-day) every six months to step back and listen again. Every time you do this you'll find new insights and be able to further refine your strategy and execution.

Listening and Assessing the Landscape

> ➤ What can you learn from listening about your business? Your competitors? Your industry? Best-in-class executors? Your target audience?
>
> ➤ Do Listen across digital touchpoints to learn as much as possible and get inspired!

_____

_____

_____

_____

_____

_____

_____

What is the big thing you want to remember from this chapter?

_____

_____

Go to www.ThatActuallyWorks.com/DigitalMarketing for your free action planner and bonus resources.

Chapter 3: Defining Your Digital Marketing Strategy: GSOT

In business and marketing we talk a lot about strategy, but what exactly is a strategy, and how do you know if it is well defined? After teaching digital marketing for years and talking about strategy I realized that most people aren't entirely sure what theirs is, the difference between a strategy, goal, or objective, or why that would matter.

Digital strategy could be its own book, but to keep focused on our goal – crafting and executing exceptional digital marketing – we'll touch on the most important things for you to know.

Think of strategy as **"how do you get what you want."** You probably know what you want at a high level – sales, sign-ups, customers, leads, patients, action, volunteers, donations, etc. – but the strategy defines the levers to pull that will get you that. **HOW** will you get what you want?

 A few years ago, I was evaluating the Facebook efforts for a hospital. They posted general health content and some stories about patients. Their stated objective for the Page was to drive traffic to their site and increase awareness.

There were two immediate issues that I saw. The first was that the content wasn't constructed well to achieve the objectives. For example, they almost never linked back to their site, so they probably were not achieving that objective.

The second issue was about the objectives. Why did they want traffic to the site, and was awareness really a concern for a hospital that has been around for so long? Could we be more specific?

In working with the marketing team we brainstormed to build a better strategy. We started with the goal = get new patients. Then we discussed the drivers of the choice of which hospital to go to. What makes someone choose a hospital? As we built this list we were building out our potential strategy list. Once we had the full list we chose 2 – 3 to focus on for the page.

The new strategy focused on building top-of-mind awareness and two brand equity perceptions - that they cared about patient health and had the best doctors in the region.

Now, with a crystal-clear strategy their Facebook content had more focus and purpose. The content strategy came to life better and the response on the Page went up. Most importantly, the marketing team could clearly show how the Facebook Page was building business value by tracking KPIs related to the strategies they chose.

Most of the thousands of businesses I've worked with of all sizes struggle to clearly define their strategy or are challenged to consistently execute against it.

Big Idea:
Regardless of where you are in crafting your strategy, this is something that can always be refined and

improved. Building a strategy that drives your business is a continuous journey.

What is marketing strategy?

According to Wikipedia:

> **Marketing strategy** has the fundamental goal of increasing sales and achieving a sustainable competitive advantage.[1] Marketing strategy includes all basic, short-term, and long-term activities in the field of marketing that deal with the analysis of the strategic initial situation of a company and the formulation, evaluation and selection of market-oriented strategies that contribute to the goals of the company and its marketing objectives.[2] *Marketing strategies* cover everything from Pay per click, search engine marketing, public relations (PR), Engineering with Marketing & the much more.

The key things to note from this definition is:
- It starts with a goal – what do you want to achieve?
- It is short-term and long-term
- It is about **how** you build an advantage and meet your goal

---

The Marketing Funnel

Having a clear strategy is so important because we know that in every industry and category sales is a process. Even seemingly impulse purchases like a pack of gum at a checkout aisle are influenced far in advance of the purchase with ads that build awareness and desire.

The marketing funnel is a foundational marketing concept that highlights the process that leads someone to buy from you. Not all purchases drive down the funnel in a linear way, but the funnel is generally true for most purchases. Some purchases spend more or less time in each stage. For example, you may spend a lot of time evaluating a car, but almost no time considering a cup of coffee. Regardless, almost all purchases happen as a result of the funnel.

Even on ecommerce sites where people can buy immediately, most people visit the site 5 – 6 times before they ultimately buy.

Example:
Imagine – it is a Friday night and you are choosing a restaurant. If you aren't aware of a restaurant it certainly can't be on your list. Once you know of it you need some level of interest – maybe you've driven by or seen your friends posting about it. Next is desire – perhaps you look up the menu online and they have some dishes that sound great. So you take action – you make the reservation and if you have a great experience you become a loyal customer and maybe even leave a review online.

Different businesses focus on different areas of the marketing funnel based on their business strategy. For example, a new restaurant may focus on awareness but an established one might focus on desire. An established consumer goods company may focus on equity around freshness (desire) but a new one may aim to build awareness or drive trial with a coupon.

Remember:
The idea is that if you focus your efforts on buying or the primary sale/conversion you will miss out on what you actually need to do to get someone to buy. If they haven't heard of you before, they probably won't trust your brand.

According to the principles of the marketing funnel, your marketing efforts should focus on one or more stages of the funnel to ultimately drive a purchase.

The Traditional Marketing Funnel

A number of years ago Google released a study called ZMOT which stands for Zero Moment of Truth. The goal of the study was to show that before making a decision, consumers conducted research online to make their decision.

The study showed that in almost all business categories consumers were influenced by 5 – 18 zero moment of truth touchpoints that influenced their purchase decision. For example, automotive shoppers sought out 18 sources of information before making a decision, for Credit Cards 9, Technology 15, Travel 10, Grocery Purchases 7, Personal Healthcare 7, and Banking 11.

The basic reality is that before taking action consumers are influenced by many aspects of your marketing – whether it is through advertising or research they conduct. As marketers we need to focus our efforts on the stages of the funnel that are most likely to grow our business in the short and long run.

Goal, Strategy, Objective, Tactic

In order to clearly define what you want to achieve, it is helpful to think in terms of **Goal, Strategy, Objective, and Tactic.** This isn't a framework that I invented; it's a common framework used in business and marketing to provide clarity around **what** you want to achieve and **how** you will achieve it.

GOAL - WHAT
The starting point is your goal – the goal is what you want to achieve. Typically this will be sales, but it could be different for a non-profit or government organization. The goal is ultimately what you want to achieve.

Example: Grow Sales 5%

STRATEGY - APPROACH
The strategy is HOW you will achieve the goal; what is the approach that you will take to drive sales? We know that choosing your business isn't as simple as action-based messaging (buy

now!!) so the strategy is the approach that you will you use achieve the goal.

Example: Increase awareness with marketing professionals.

OBJECTIVES – MEASURABLE STEPS
What are the specific measurable steps that you will take to achieve the goal based on the strategy? It's best if these are specific, but don't get too caught up in the numbers if you don't have a good benchmark. Focus on the result that you want to get.

Example: Reach 50K digital marketers on our site and 500K off-site through advertising

TACTICS – ACTIONS
What are the actions that you will take to achieve the objectives? This is where you get into the execution. You can also tie KPIs (Key Performance Indicators) to your tactics or actions to know what your target is. This is helpful to determine if you have an appropriate budget or plan to achieve the objectives that you set.

Example: Blog posts – KPI 1K users/week; Facebook Ads – Reach 1K @$3CPM, etc.

Working within the GSOT framework is vital if you want success. Most businesses are clear on their goal and their tactics, but often the strategy and objectives become muddled or unclear, which may limit your success.

I had been promoting myself as an expert and speaker for many years online. I had a clear goal to book more paid speaking engagements. I would use clear tactics of being active on Facebook, Twitter, LinkedIn, etc. If you had asked my strategy I would have said that by building awareness about myself as a subject matter expert I would gain more speaking engagements over time. The reality was I didn't have a well thought-out strategy.

After teaching a class on strategy I decided to get serious about my own. Who were the people who booked speakers and how could I get in front of them? I came up with the strategy (approach) to target meeting and event planners online. My objective was to gain visibility with them as a social media expert. I used my blog and LinkedIn very deliberately to reach this group. As a result, I booked paid gigs and landed webinars with the biggest meeting and event planner organization in the globe.

If you are really intentional about HOW you will achieve your goal you can create more focused efforts. By using only two digital marketing tools strategically I gained more results faster than in my five years of using them with a vague strategy.

Remember:
This is a process. You may not have all the answers exactly right immediately. Most businesses create and revise their strategies annually or periodically throughout the year. Come up with your best ideas for now and move forward. You can revisit and refine over time, but don't let not having the answers hold you back from acting.

Defining Your Goal

Defining the goal is usually pretty straightforward for most businesses – the goal is ultimately what you want to achieve with your efforts. Depending on the size and scale of your organization or business, your goal could be broad or specific.

For example, a goal could be to grow sales, which is broad, but a solid goal for an annual marketing plan. A more specific goal could be to drive sales of a new product launch. Either one works for the purpose of building your strategy. Think about what you want to achieve for your brand or business, and that should be your goal.

Sample Goals:
- Grow sales
- Increase donations
- Gain volunteers
- Drive sales of a new product
- Increase sales of a specific product
- Sign-ups for an event
- Awareness of a program
- Change a behavior
- Change perceptions

The goal is the high-level thing that you want to get from your efforts. Even if you work for a government organization or nonprofit where you aren't selling a product, you should have a clear goal.

Defining Your Strategies

Your strategy is how you will approach achieving your goal – and depending on your organization size and budget you can have 1 – 4 strategies. Keep in mind that the more strategies you have the less focused your efforts will be.

Your **digital strategy** should identify your approach at using digital marketing to achieve your goal. Different businesses use different strategies based on the nature of their product or service, as well as their position in the marketplace.

For example, at Boot Camp Digital, where we sell digital marketing training, we use different strategies for our different products.

For our B2B sales of corporate training programs we rely on conversion as our primary strategy. We focus on getting and converting qualified leads. Since the service is relatively specific and we have limited resources, we focus exclusively on leads. Could we benefit from other parts of the marketing funnel? Of course! But with limited resources we need to focus. After we master our lead conversion strategy we may expand up or down the funnel.

For our public training programs (online training courses and live open-enrollment Boot Camps) we focus on awareness and nurturing more. We want to make people aware of our programs and the value that they bring.

Having a clear strategy helps us to prioritize our efforts and focus. Your strategies can and should shift over time as the market evolves.

Digital marketing strategies broadly fall into five categories: Attract/Reach, Nurture, Convert, Retain & Grow and Advocate.

Attract/Reach – This strategy focuses on building awareness of your product or service offering. This is usually a strategy for businesses or products that are not well known in the marketplace. The idea here is to get in front of people in your target audience so that they will think of you when they need your product.

For example, a new restaurant may aim to build awareness to become part of your decision-set when you think of where to eat.

Nurture – This strategy is about creating a favorable impression about your product or service. In traditional marketing this would be considered brand equity or positioning. Your objective is to create a specific impression about your brand, product, or service.

For example, a restaurant wants to be known for the best cheesecake in the city.

Convert – The goal of conversion is to drive someone to act now and transact with you. While most businesses ultimately want to convert, it is important to keep in mind that attract and nurture are usually required in order to do so – few purchases are made immediately without brand awareness or equity.

For example, a restaurant sends out coupons or promotes their happy hour to get people in the door.

Retain and Grow – Most businesses spend most of their energy in marketing acquiring new customers, but increasing revenue from existing customers is often an easier strategy to execute with better return on investment. The idea here is to focus marketing efforts on gaining additional purchases or larger purchases from existing customers.

For example, a restaurant may have a loyalty program, or give first-time diners a special offer for their next visit.

Advocate – Word-of-mouth is a top driver for almost every business, but many businesses don't spend any time or effort driving it or advocacy. While word-of-mouth is often a bi-product of exceptional service, smart businesses engineer it into their product and touchpoints with customers. Advocacy as a marketing strategy aims at generating recommendations, referrals, and word-of-mouth around your product or service.

For example, a restaurant may have an Instagram contest or hashtag promoted on the menu or at tables.

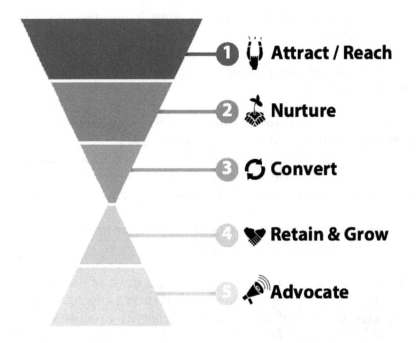

1. Attract / Reach
2. Nurture
3. Convert
4. Retain & Grow
5. Advocate

As you can see, any business could easily use all five steps as a part of their marketing execution, however based on their specific challenges in driving sales they may choose specific strategies that are most likely to grow their sales in the short and long run.

Remember:
Even though your goal is typically to drive conversions, successful marketing relies on knowing what it takes to drive the conversions that you want. Don't get too focused on driving conversions that you forget about the strategies that support conversions over time.

Defining Your Objectives

An objective is a specific and measurable thing that you want to achieve – your tactics will support you in achieving this. An objective is specifically what you want to get as a result of your strategy. Different strategies will lend themselves to different objectives.

Ideally a strong objective should be specific and have a number attached to it, like generate 5% more leads. That being said, if you are new to digital marketing it may be difficult to set goals. Your goal should also link to your budget or resources dedicated to executing against the objective. Don't get too caught up in the numbers if you aren't sure – aim to improve.

Big Idea:
Many businesses get caught up on benchmarks and trying to assign targets to their objectives. If you don't have any historical performance, it can be very challenging to set realistic benchmarks. Focus on improving.

Sample objectives for different marketing strategies are below. Each of these should have a specific number or percentage increase assigned to it to make is measurable.

Awareness
- Reach a certain number of people
- Views of your videos
- Increase new visitors to site
- Reach new people on social networks
- Grow organic traffic to site
- Build following on social networks
- Reach target conference attendees

Nurture
- Traffic to blog posts
- Email sign-ups
- Email opens
- Website traffic

- Reduce bounce rate
- Increase return visitors
- Traffic to target articles
- Downloads of resources
- Views of video tutorials
- Reach on retargeted ads

Convert
- Leads
- Sales
- Increase online sales
- Grow coupon downloads
- Increase lead-generation form completions
- Increase phone calls
- Increase clicks on direct purchase search ads

Retain
- Increase cart size
- Return customers
- Improve open + click rates on customer emails
- Improve response rates of customer follow-up calls
- Reach customers with new product offers

Advocate
- Mentions
- Reviews
- Positive mentions
- Use of promoted or branded hashtags
- Increase social shares of content
- Gain mentions from influencers
- Increase digital PR
- Increase mentions on blogs

The objective should measurably define what you want to happen. Sometimes an objective can be delivered with a single tactic, but often times it is a combination of tactics that work together to achieve a goal. For example, generating leads requires a strong website/lead form plus a strategy to drive qualified leads to the site which may include advertising, organic posting, and content.

By knowing your objective you can evaluate your tactics based on their ability to achieve it.

Defining Your Tactics

Part 2 of this book is dedicated to a deep dive on digital marketing tactics. Once you understand your goal, strategy, and objectives you should be able to choose the digital marketing tools that are most likely to drive your business.

There is almost no end to what you **could do** in digital marketing; the question is what you **should do.** Prioritizing your efforts and executing with excellence is the key to your success.

Understanding the range of digital tactics available to you and how they work and can contribute to your objective is the first step. Prioritizing and focusing your efforts based on your goal, strategy, and objectives is the second.

Goals   Strategy   Objectives   Tactics

Putting Your GSOT Together

With digital we have the opportunity to be more specific in our objective, which leads to a more focused outcome. For example, with ad targeting on Facebook, Google, YouTube, LinkedIn, and almost any other digital medium starts with the **objective** of the ad. The ad will then be optimized to best achieve that objective. Each ad can only have one objective, so it's important to be focused and clear on the primary goal of the ad.

Big Idea:
Defining your strategy and objectives are more important in digital vs. traditional because digital marketing has more options. For example, if you want to place a television or magazine ad you are buying the same ad regardless of your marketing objective. Your creative will vary, but the way you buy and target the audience is the same because the media is mass focused.

While having a clear strategy is helpful in traditional marketing, it is vital in digital because of the precision with which we can execute.

Once you have put your GSOT together, you should be able to create a chart, similar to the one below where each tactic clearly leads to an objective that clearly ties to a strategy. KPIs (Key Performance Indicators used to measure results) can be set at the objective and the tactical levels. Setting KPIs at both levels helps you to see if your tactics are sufficient to achieve your objective.

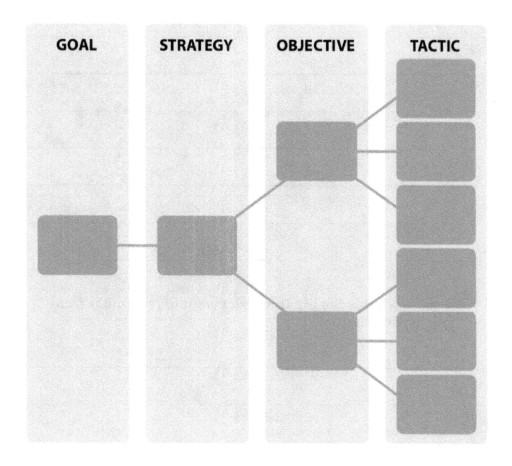

Defining Your Digital Marketing Strategy

- ➢ What is your goal?
- ➢ What are your strategies to achieve the goal?
- ➢ What are your objectives?
- ➢ What metrics will indicate your success?

_____

_____

_____

_____

_____

_____

_____

What is the big thing you want to remember from this chapter?

_____

_____

Go to www.ThatActuallyWorks.com/DigitalMarketing for your free action planner and bonus resources.

Chapter 4: Target Audience

Defining your target audience is important in your marketing strategy in general, but it's even more important in digital because it leads to better results.

For example, in running an ad on Facebook you can target not just by demographics and location but also by behaviors and interests. By really understanding the people that you want to reach you can better use digital marketing tools to get in front of them.

Narrowing Your Audience

Defining your audience as specifically as possible will make your digital marketing more impactful as you can be more strategic in your approach.

Many businesses define their target broadly based on demographics. For example, "Women between 30 and 50 with two children who want the best for their family." This is a pretty vague definition of a target audience. Who doesn't want the best for their family?

We often hesitate to define our target audience specifically because we don't want to *limit* our reach. I'm guilty of this with my own business – it is so hard to focus because so many people can benefit from our products!

But if we try to speak to everyone we'll speak to nobody. Many small business marketing coaches preach, "the riches are in the niches." Meaning you can build a more sustainable business by truly being the best at something specific vs. trying to do many things.

When you define your target audience, try to focus in on who you really solve a problem for.

 I started my career working on Tide laundry detergent brand. While many people use Tide (it had almost 50% market share) the brand didn't target everyone. Tide had the best cleaning detergent on the market, and their target audience could be defined as soccer moms – moms with two children, a dog, and a minivan living in the suburbs. These moms have to get real stains out of clothes and they want the clothes to look great.

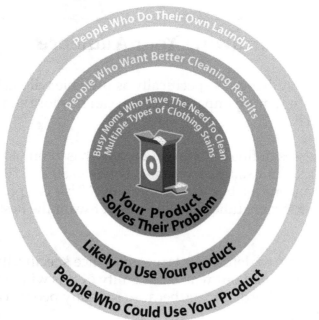

Define your audience as specifically as possible based on who you are solving a real problem for.

Understanding Your Audience

Once you know who you really want to reach, try to understand this audience in as much detail as possible. There are many very specific targeting options online, and the better you know your audience the better you will be able to target them.

Many businesses don't take full advantage of digital because they aren't able to harness the targeting options available.

Identify the following for your target audience:

- Age
- Gender
- Location
- Other demographics
- Interests
- Profession
- Behaviors

Tool: Facebook Audience Insights
If you already have a digital presence, consider using **Facebook Audience Insights** (facebook.com/ads/audience_insights) to learn more about your target audience. Discover other Pages they like, their interests, and more.

Where Is Your Audience Online?
Explore where your audience is online. Learn about them as much as possible.

Some of the questions to ask are:

- What news sites do they go to?
- What discussion forums do they participate in?
- Are there niche community sites?
- What social networks are they active on?
- What do they do on each social network and how active are they?
- What sharing sites are they active on?
- Do they have groups on these sites?
- Are there niche online groups that they are a part of?
- What blogs do they read?
- Who are the influential bloggers?
- Who is influential on Twitter?
- Who are the community leaders?
- Are they members of organizations?
- What social news sites are they a part of?

What Do They Talk About?

After understanding where they are online, gain an understanding of what they talk about. What are the subject areas they are passionate about and interested in? What areas do they have questions about? Look at other blogs or news sites in your industry – what stories or articles get the most comments or are the most popular? Understanding what they want to talk about is the next important step to a larger understanding of your target audience.

 When I got started in digital I worked at a photography website start-up where we spent a lot of time online trying to understand what our target audience was interested in. We developed two key insights. The first was that they were very passionate about photographers' rights as there were tons of posts about this topic. The second was that they had lots of legal questions.

We used these two insights to develop a content strategy that linked to the business of selling photographs (what our business did) while creating content our audience was passionate about. In a few months we had one of the most popular photography blogs online by tapping into what our audience was interested in.

Using Personas

Creating personas of your buyers or customers is a great way to gain an even deeper understanding of your target audience. Looking at your potential "buyers" or customers as complete people. Painting an image of them will help you execute your digital marketing more effectively. Most businesses will have multiple personas, as there are different use-cases for their product or service.

According to Wikipedia::

Personas are fictional characters created to represent the different user types within a targeted demographic, attitude and/or behavior set that might use a brand or product in a similar way. Personas are a tool or method of market segmentation.

Personas are useful in considering the goals, desires, and limitations of brand buyers and users in order to help to guide decisions about a service, product, or interaction space such as features, interactions, and visual design of a website.

Essentially, a buyer persona is a detailed profile of an example buyer that represents the real audience. Beyond demographic information, it includes their behavior, interests, goals, skills, attitudes, family and life situation, hobbies, etc. The goal is to create an actual person who represents your target audience. By thinking about the needs of a fictitious persona, marketers and designers are better able to infer the interests of a real per- son in a given situation.

Politicians in their campaigns often use personas. Bill Clinton and George W. Bush both campaigned to "soccer moms" during the elections. The presidents' campaign staff uses dozens of personas like these to help focus their message and earn more votes.

In the 2008 election, Republican Vice President Nominee Sarah Palin famously referred to "Joe Six-Pack and Hockey Moms" during a debate and the Presidential Candidate John McCain referenced "Joe the Plumber" when talking about how tax plans could hurt average Americans.

The political references are not intended to get into a discussion about political marketing, rather they are used to highlight the universal use of personas in examples that most people are familiar with.

A persona essentially is a description of who you are trying to reach and how your product helps them.

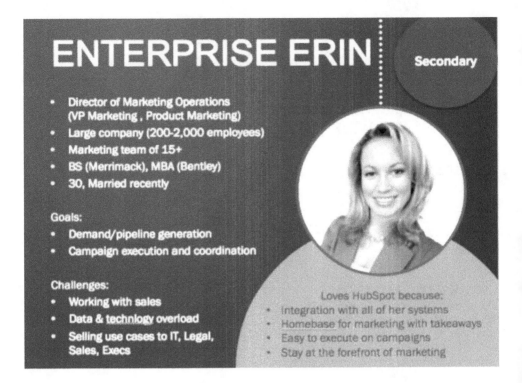

For success in digital marketing, it is vital to have a deep understanding of your target consumer, so you can develop compelling and relevant content.

Action:
Solidify as much as you know about your target audiences and create personas of the main types of people who buy from you, as well as their goals and motivations.

Target Audience

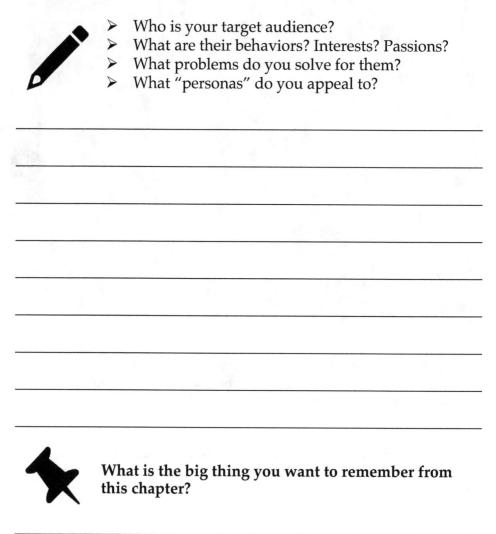

> ➤ Who is your target audience?
> ➤ What are their behaviors? Interests? Passions?
> ➤ What problems do you solve for them?
> ➤ What "personas" do you appeal to?

_____

_____

_____

_____

_____

_____

_____

_____

What is the big thing you want to remember from this chapter?

_____

_____

Go to www.ThatActuallyWorks.com/DigitalMarketing for your
free action planner and bonus resources.

Chapter 5: Digital Content

Content is a topic that is relevant to any digital marketing tool. Whether you plan to have a website, an email campaign, run ads, or participate in social media, content will be a key part of your success.

Since the beginning of digital marketing and social media, experts and gurus have preached that "content is king." Of course it is. That would be like saying the television commercial you create is the most important part of your television strategy. Of course it is.

With digital however, there are a few reasons that we need to think even more strategically about digital content.

5 Keys to Crafting Compelling Digital Content

1. **Focus on Content Over Technology**
   With digital marketing many businesses get so focused on the technology or the technical aspects of implementation that they forget about the content. Many businesses who run Facebook Ads spend tons of time focused on the audience and budget, but the actual posts perform poorly, so their money is being wasted. Businesses rush to create chatbots without first understanding what their customers may want from them on this channel.

Shift your focus in digital to the content.

2. **Consumer Value**
   In most traditional marketing we focus on brand value –
   does the creative effectively sell our product or service. This
   was because we were paying for a set impression with
   people. In digital marketing people can choose to pay
   attention or ignore you. There are fewer "forced view"
   mediums, so smart brands focus on creating content that
   consumers *want* to view or interact with.

   This is true for all digital channels. If people don't like your
   website or find it difficult to use, they'll move on. If your
   email subject line is no good, they won't open it. If your
   email doesn't inspire them, they won't click, or they'll
   unsubscribe. If your Facebook ad is boring, they'll scroll by.
   If you don't entice them, they don't give their email address.

   Content for digital must be consumer-centric in order to
   drive attention and ultimately achieve your business
   objectives.

   Think consumer first.

3. **Break Through Clutter and Noise**
   People are more distracted than ever before and have more
   messages (both advertising and otherwise) targeted at them
   every day. With the proliferation of social media, people can
   be exposed to thousands of updates from their friends a day
   – just on Facebook.

   In order to break through the clutter and stand out your
   content must have thumb-stopping power. It must attract
   attention and drive someone to stop and pay attention.

   Think thumb-stopping power in your content.

4. **Branding Matters**

   In addition to having thumb-stopping user value, your content also needs to have brand or business value – immediately present. Some marketers think that if your content contains too much branding that people will scroll through and it won't have the thumb-stopping power to draw people in.

   The reality is that great content integrates brands in natural and authentic ways. Over-branding and over-logoing content is definitely a turn off to consumers, but naturally integrating your brand isn't.

   Integrate your brand naturally in context.

5. **Speed**

   People are more distracted and consume more content more quickly than ever before. Images and visuals are arising as the key digital content as a result of this – because they communicate more information more quickly vs. text.

   Facebook talks about the "speed of feed" and highlights that people spend under two seconds on each post on mobile devices. On websites people spend an average of 6 – 8 seconds on homepages. This means that we need to communicate quickly and efficiently. Think about how to bite-size your message and prioritize what is really important to communicate to create digital content.

   Make all of your messages short, clear, and simple. Reduce the number of communication points and focus on a single clear message to allow someone to quickly understand your point. More is just more and will lead to you getting lost in the noise.

   Make messages instantly understandable and short.

If it sounds tough to achieve all of the items listed above, it is! Combining these elements requires creative and strategic thinking – and it may take time and testing to find the best way to bring your message to life in the digital space.

Remember:
These content optimization tips apply to any digital channel in any format. Always assume that people are busy, they aren't inherently interested in you, and you have to break through a noisy marketplace where they are only going to give you a few seconds to capture their attention.

Brand Value and User Value

The key to great digital content is finding the right mix of brand value and user value. **Brand value** means that the content is strategically created to build the brand. **User value** means that it is interesting to the consumer.

Missing Brand Value
If a post is really interesting to people but the brand is minimized or not present, it isn't meeting your business objectives. So while people may like it, it won't ultimately grow your business.

A great example of this is Taco Bell. Many years ago Taco Bell launched an ad campaign that people loved featuring a Chihuahua that said "Yo Quiero Taco Bell". The campaign was so popular that sales of Chihuahuas went up and Taco Bell sold stuffed dogs. But sales were flat, because the dog, while cute, didn't make people want to eat Taco Bell. When Taco Bell switched back to product-focused commercials their sales rebounded.

Missing User Value

At the same time, if your post isn't interesting to people it won't have a big impact in digital. People quickly scroll through content on digital channels and eye-tracking studies show that we are great at avoiding ads that aren't of interest. Brands need to earn attention by creating content that is valuable to people.

 Brand lift studies from Facebook show that content that isn't interesting to people can have little impact on branding. If your ad is boring people scroll by so quickly it barely makes an impression, and it becomes more expensive as Facebook doesn't want to show ads that people don't like. On websites as well, people will leave quickly if they don't find value from your site.

Balance Brand Value and User Value

Marketers sometimes feel that these objectives are at odds with each other – that if digital content has branding in it, it won't be interesting to people. This is not the case, and in fact neither Google nor Facebook have studies that suggest this. The most effective posts for brands integrate the branding in a natural way.

When you evaluate your content on any digital channel evaluate it against these two concepts.

20/60/20 Content Mix

Regardless of the digital tools that you choose to employ to achieve your objectives, it is usually helpful at the outset to give some thought to your content strategy. What content can you share that will be both interesting to your target audience and also make them more likely to buy from you or achieve whatever other goal you have set?

Krista Neher

As you start to think about your content, it's helpful to consider what makes great content and where you want to be. The best content should aim at being both interesting to your audience and promotional of your business. That being said, you may have some content that is purely promotional and some that is less promotional but highly relevant to your audience.

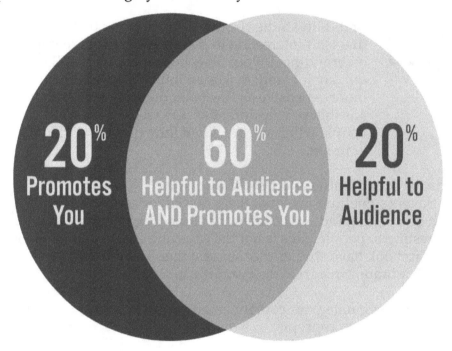

Ideally, the aim of creating content should be to move each piece as close to the center as possible. Even if you have a purely promotional message, ask yourself how you can make it interesting to someone? What stats or surprise facts are there around it? What makes it sharable?

Example:
Holidays and events are a great example of topics that people are interested in so brands create content around them (Happy Easter, Happy Mother's Day, etc.) but many brands struggle with making the

holiday relevant for their brand. Instead of just posting "Happy Whatever Day" – think about how it relates to or connects with your business in a meaningful way that is interesting to your audience. This will take your content from mediocre to thumb-stopping.

Design for Mobile

When it comes to digital content, we need to design for mobile, unless you have a desktop specific application. Most marketers know this – we hear it all the time – but we don't do a great job of implementing it.

On almost every digital channel – websites, social, search, ads – mobile is overtaking desktop as the primary delivery channel. If you aren't sure if your industry follows this trend, take a quick look at your analytics.

 Power Tip:
Be sure to evaluate all of your creative on a mobile phone. Make sure that it's simple, clear, and digestible in only a few seconds to work well in the fast-moving mobile space.

Defining Your Content Strategy

Your content strategy is essentially about defining what you will post when. The specifics of frequency and content optimization will depend largely on the channels that you use, however it is often helpful upfront to create a general idea of the different types of content that you will create.

Your content strategy will be heavily based on your marketing strategy and objectives, as well as your target audience. Keep these in mind as you start to build your strategy.

Power Tip:
If you are struggling with your content topics or feel that your content isn't interesting enough, go back to the listening stage to get ideas! Look at great content that is relevant to your business on Pinterest, Instagram, YouTube, Twitter, and blogs to get inspired by some of the best content creators in the world.

The first step in building your content strategy is to define the content topics that are relevant for your business. It is usually helpful to have 5 – 10 content topics, although you could have fewer.

You may start with a large list and refine it down over time. For example, an ice cream company may have a content topic list including:

- Food porn (ice cream you are dying to eat)
- Recipes
- Emotional posts (eg. eating ice cream when you are sad)
- Current events
- Joy of ice cream (kids-focused)
- Promotions (sales, new products)
- Ingredients/natural focus

The topics can be refined over time as you gain experience. Don't think of them as a set list forever, but more as a starting point. You will also note in the list above that most of the topics are relevant for the customer and the brand, however a few are more self-serving for the business. It's good to have a mix of content at this point.

Power Tip:
As you define the content topics that are relevant to you it can be helpful to think about the full marketing funnel, especially for channels like your website where visitors are in varying stages in their willingness to buy from you. Some may be ready to convert while others are just getting to know you. Once you've developed your content buckets ask yourself if you have covered the entire funnel.

Example:
Looking at the website for Sephora, a beauty company, we can see a variety of content topics present representing the entire marketing funnel.

- Attract – How-To content
- Nurture – Community, Gifts, Inspiration
- Convert – Shop
- Retention– Community
- Advocacy – Stories

Sephora is a large global business with significant marketing budget, so over time they have been able to create meaningful content across the funnel. Depending on your business maturity and budget you may focus on only one stage.

As you execute in digital marketing you will use different content on different channels. In the ice cream example, they may post emotional photos and joy of ice cream on Instagram but focus Pinterest on recipes. Their website may heavily focus on ingredients and promotions. Later, as you build your channel strategy you'll determine which content belongs where.

Action Item:
Define your content buckets that you can bring to life across digital channels. Consider if you are representing the entire funnel and explore the content that your audience is really interested in.

Keep in mind that as you execute you'll learn more about the content that performs best. Also recognize that content works in trends. For example five years ago inspirational quotes were really popular on many channels, and now we find they aren't achieving the same success.

Define the Content Medium

As we review digital channels we'll dive in to best practices per channel, but for the most part, what it takes to create powerful digital content by medium is similar across channels. Within any channel you will usually find a combination of text, images, and video. For example, all three are heavily used on Facebook. A website will also usually include all three types of content.

Big Idea:
The principles below may not apply 100% to every channel, and some industries are different. For

example, in some B2B industries longer content (both text and video) out-performs because people are highly interested in the topic. Be sure to confirm that these best practices work for your business by testing and looking at analytics to see what your audience responds best to.

Text
Text is usually a component of any digital media post. Even a YouTube video has a text title and description. Below are some best practices for digital text that applies to most mediums.

- Shorter is better
- Get to the point quickly
- Organize content with headers, bullets, emojis, etc.
- Aim for a single communication method
- If you want something, ask for It explicitly
- Eliminate extra detail
- Establish a clear value proposition
- Draw people in with a compelling headline
- Think in terms of the audience – what's in it for them?
- Resist the urge to always explain everything
- Consider short and fun – let people read between the lines

Images
Images and design have been a key part of digital executions from the beginning. Use images strategically.

Below are some best practices for images.

- Clear and clean visuals
- Use white-space
- Limit text in a visual
- Clear single focus point
- Consistent with your brand

- Use brand assets (colors, logo, design elements) strategically
- Don't over-brand content with logos and design elements everywhere
- Visually stunning that draws people in
- Contextually relevant
- Real photos can work well
- Avoid overly fake looking stock photos
- Make the picture worth a thousand words.

Power Tip:
Let your images do the heavy lifting. Choose visuals that describe what you want to communicate – make your pictures worth a thousand words.

Videos:
There are now SO MANY different styles and formats of videos. From Live videos to YouTube bumper ads, we see more videos in more places than ever before. Videos are becoming more prominent on every social network and almost every medium.

- Have a clear and compelling storyline
- Grab attention immediately
- Brand or business present in context
- Flexible format – horizontal for YouTube, vertical for Facebook and Instagram
- Branding present from the beginning (ideally in context and not just a logo)
- Fast-paced
- High action – lots of cuts and movements
- Check sound – it should work with or without sound when possible
- Lighting matters
- Consider the design look and feel of the video
- Start strong – capture attention immediately
- Show the payoff or the big idea first

- Single, clear message – don't try to do too much

Google and Facebook have done research on how to create a compelling story arc for digital. In traditional marketing, the video usually starts off slow, maybe even with a logo build. Next there's a reveal and usually the brand at the end.

In digital we need to grab attention quickly and maintain it. We need to start with the big excitement or the payout. Consider recipe videos – they START by showing you the END - the mouthwatering food that you will learn to make.

The image below demonstrates a traditional video story-arc compared to a digital one. Digital and traditional storytelling are quite different.

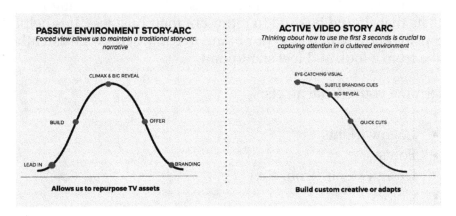

 Remember: Once you get started you'll learn from your audience what works and what doesn't. Don't invest too much upfront if you aren't sure what your audience will respond to. Be agile, try a few things, analyze, and build on those results.

Tone of Voice & Style Guides

Prior to diving in to digital it can be helpful to be sure that you have strong style guides and a distinctive tone-of-voice for your business.

Power Tip:
Spending time upfront defining your tone of voice and general style guidelines will make it easier to execute consistently on digital. With so many assets being created, and comments being responded to, having a clear idea of how you want to come across will save you time in the long-run.

Many businesses have brand guidelines – the colors and logo formats that should be used to represent their business. It is helpful to consider how you want your brand to come across consistently online from a look and feel standpoint.

Determine your visual assets:
- Logo
- Logo variants
- Fonts
- Design assets (icon, etc.)
- Colors

Prior to jumping in it can be helpful to determine your tone of voice:
- What should the brand sound like?
- Are you funny or serious?
- What is your distinctive voice?
- What visual assets can you use?
- How will you handle controversy?
- What do you stand for?

Some businesses find it helpful to find a celebrity that embodies their brand. This can be a simple test of your content to ask – would this person say it in that way?

Action Item:
Establish some quick tone-of-voice and visual guidelines for your brand or business. These could be longer and well established if you work for a large brand, or quickly written down for a small business or startup. Be sure that you have a **distinctive** tone of voice so your brand starts to consistently build an impression with your consumers.

Digital Content

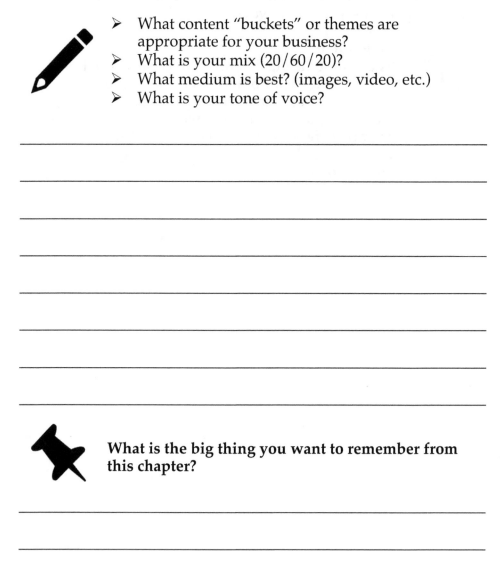

> ➤ What content "buckets" or themes are appropriate for your business?
> ➤ What is your mix (20/60/20)?
> ➤ What medium is best? (images, video, etc.)
> ➤ What is your tone of voice?

_____

_____

_____

_____

_____

_____

_____

What is the big thing you want to remember from this chapter?

_____

_____

Go to www.ThatActuallyWorks.com/DigitalMarketing for your free action planner and bonus resources.

PART 2: DIGITAL MARKETING CHANNELS

There are new digital channels emerging regularly. The biggest challenge for marketers is to determine which digital marketing tools to use to most efficiently and effectively achieve their marketing goals.

While it seems that there are new technologies every day, the reality is that the core digital marketing tools that marketers have relied on for years continue to be the big levers driving business.

The question isn't what you **could** do it is what you **should** do. Almost any channel or tool could be used by almost any business.

The goal in building a digital marketing strategy is to better understand the digital tools that are most likely to grow your business, based on your objectives, and to use them effectively.

We identify eight primary digital marketing tools that are used by most businesses: Social Media, Digital Ads, SEO (Search Engine Optimization), Websites, Conversational Marketing, Email, CRM, and Mobile.

Each of these tools could easily be an entire book on their own. My goal in the coming section is to help you understand what each one is, how it works, how to strategically use it for business, and some best practices to help you execute with excellence.

Don't be too distracted by shiny new digital platforms. In order to be effective they need to develop a solid platform for advertisers and marketers and also have mass adoption so you aren't just speaking to an empty room.

Chapter 6: Social Media Marketing

Social media has been a major digital marketing channel for the last decade, but there have been some dramatic shifts that have changed how social media fits into marketing strategies.

Social media is no longer new, but businesses are still working to improve how they use social networks to connect with their customers. As social media has become more mature as a marketing platform we now have gone beyond questioning the its value and now focus on how it fits into our strategy and how to use best practices and innovation to get better results.

Trends in Social Media Marketing

Algorithm Driven

The first big trend in social media marketing is that now most social networks are algorithm driven. This means that people don't see the latest posts in their news feed – they see the posts that the network believes they are most likely to be interested in.

In some cases business content gets reduced exposure (on Facebook) but most algorithms are designed to show you the best content for you based on your affinity for the person or page posting (how often you seem to like their content), how the post itself is performing, and how recent the post is.

Note: This is why you tend to see posts from the same handful of people on Facebook, even though you have hundreds of friends.

Facebook started this trend but it's now true on most social networks like Twitter, Instagram, and LinkedIn.

The bottom line is that if you want to break through on social media you need exceptional content.

Great Content Matters

With more and more noise on social networks, you need great content to break through and be heard. Even if you run an ad, if people don't its content, it will become more expensive or stop running.

Marketers have a huge challenge on social media to create great content that has thumb-stopping power and drives impact.

In the early days of social media we used to talk a lot about calendars and frequency. These days **quality** is more important than **quantity.** Social media marketers are posting less often but focusing on higher quality content when they do post.

Video, Video, Video

Video is HUGE on almost all social networks and growing quickly. Several years ago, Facebook and other networks started to really emphasize video as the key content they wanted to encourage.

Video posts usually get more views vs. text, image, or link posts and since people pause to watch your video you are getting a higher quality engagement or impression.

The types of videos that you can create and the interactivity within them is also growing constantly. There are now Live videos on most social networks, Watch or TV networks to encourage longer-format syndication, and interactive video elements like polls, stickers, and clickable elements appearing.

If video isn't a part of your social media strategy it should be.

Advertising

Advertising is now becoming a staple of most social media strategies. It used to be that social media was considered "organic" – meaning people would naturally see your content if it was great.

As a result of the lack of organic traction, more and more brands are relying on advertising, which isn't a bad thing. Many marketers are outraged that social networks want businesses to pay but really, if your message is worth creating and sharing it should be worth advertising.

Social media advertising is incredibly easy and low cost for businesses to get started. It doesn't require big bucks and, in fact, many small, smart, and nimble companies are out performing billion dollar brands.

Stories

Stories as a format for social media is growing big time. While at the moment Stories are limited to only a few platforms (and arguably copy Snapchat) it is expected that this news feed format will continue to grow.

If you aren't familiar with Stories you can see them on both Facebook and Instagram. Stories are a sort of full-screen news feed where the entire picture or video takes over your screen and you can tap to move to the next one.

Stories are highly visual – mostly images, short text, or short videos – and tend to be more fun and playful. They have stickers, lenses, and fun camera effects to play with.

Stories are the fastest growing product in Facebook history (Yes, faster than Instagram and Messenger!) and Mark Zuckerberg believes that Stories will be the future of the news feed.

If you haven't started playing with Stories yet, start now. Businesses can create organic stories or story ads.

There is No Next Big Thing

For the longest time in social media we were all looking for "the next big thing" – mostly because early movers could gain a significant advantage by getting big on a social network first.

What we've seen now is that there are a handful of established players and breaking in is incredibly difficult. The failure of Google+, a social network launched by Google, showed that people are happy to stay where their friends are.

The other trend we've seen is that when new players emerge rather than moving to the new platform the big social networks just figure out how to integrate that functionality.

A number of years ago live streaming was launched by apps called Periscope and Meerkat. Early adopters joined these sites but, within a year, Twitter acquired Periscope, and Facebook and YouTube launched Live as a type of video.

The "next big thing" will probably come from the big networks and be more about in-platform innovation.

The Social Media Landscape

In the early days of social media, we had a variety of complex graphics to discuss the social media landscape with hundreds (if not thousands) of businesses.

Now, social media has matured and there are a handful of big players that most businesses focus on. The rate of change has slowed and a presence on social media is an expectation for most businesses.

When it comes to social networks there are six main platforms that most businesses consider participating in.

You may argue that Snapchat should be included, however the size remains small relative to the more established networks. From a business standpoint the Snapchat audience heavily overlaps with Instagram so most businesses find it more efficient to reach the audience on Instagram.

CHOOSING THE RIGHT SOCIAL MEDIA PLATFORM FOR YOUR BUSINESS					
2.06 billion users	**1** billion users	**20** million users	**1.5** billion users	**530** million registered users	**200** million users
Everyone	Mainstream & young users	A mix of experts and commons	Almost everyone	Professionals	Very niche, but very loyal
Images & Videos	Images & Videos	Text, Links, GIFs, Short Video	Video	Short Blogs, Infographics, Images & Videos	Images, Infographics
Solid – Best in the business	Excellent, courtesy Facebook	Decent	Robust platform High ROI	Strong – ROI not up to the mark	Good if targeted well
Clickbait & Fake News	Limited user attention span	Lack of security against trolls and abusers	Videos can be expensive to make	Largely focused on careers and jobs	Very niche demographics

A summary overview of the main social networks:

Facebook – The largest and most established social network. With so many people spending so much time on Facebook, it is the natural first choice for many businesses. Even B2B companies often find it easier to reach a business audience on Facebook vs. LinkedIn because people are so engaged there. More and more, a Facebook presence is an expectation for businesses.

Instagram – Owned by Facebook, Instagram has continued to grow steadily, and the visual format leads to high engagement rates. The Instagram audience does skew younger vs. average population. Instagram is powerful for visual businesses, yet many businesses still aren't as active as they could be on the platform. The rise of Instagram Influencers also means that many businesses rely on partners to promote them on Instagram. Currently, and according to Instagram, there is no extra feed presence given to either personal or business accounts, so business accounts can still get a ton of organic reach.

Twitter – Twitter is one of the oldest social networks and these days it seems to struggle to find its place in the social media world. Twitter still has a large and engaged user base and is heavily used for interest-based topics – like politics, entertainment, hobbies, and B2B categories. Twitter can be a challenge for businesses because it takes more time and effort vs. other networks, but the payoffs can be big if your audience starts to interact with you there.

YouTube – You could argue whether or not YouTube is a social network, but the reality is that tons of people watch and interact with videos on YouTube every day. As video becomes a medium of choice for people and businesses YouTube is again highly relevant and continues to drive business. Possibly YouTube is more of a syndication platform vs. a social network. Mastering YouTube can result in millions of video views for your business.

LinkedIn – LinkedIn is still **the business network.** Nothing else comes close, and since the acquisition by Microsoft they've gotten more serious about rolling out new innovative features for users and businesses. Every business should have some presence on LinkedIn, but B2B businesses should see it as a strategic tool. With a renewed focus on the news feed, content, videos, and groups, LinkedIn is positioning itself as a bigger and more relevant business platform.

Pinterest – Pinterest is still privately owned and arguably not as broadly popular as the other big networks. It is still large and growing and importantly, shows tremendous potential for businesses to organically promote their content. Pinterest is the go-to website for recipes, style, home décor, weddings, food, shopping, design, and fitness. What makes Pinterest unique is that people are sharing content from the Internet. Over 80% of Pins are repins – which means that it is where people go to share and discover things they are interested in.

Blogs – While not a social network, blogs are usually included in social media marketing. Blogs are often considered a type of social media because of the commenting features and how readers can engage as part of a community. A blog is a website or a part of a website that is characterized by content that is updated regularly and displayed with newest content first. Businesses have blogs as a way to share their thought-leadership and expertise with their audience, and to act as a hub to draw people to their websites. Blogs also have significant benefits for SEO or search engine optimization.

Power Tip:
If you are planning to create profiles on multiple social networks, create a central email account to register all of your profiles. This way all accounts are tied to an email that can be accessed by multiple people in the organization vs. an individual (who may leave).

Social Media Strategies and Approaches

As social networks have evolved there are a number of different approaches that businesses use.

Big Idea:
Keep in mind you will get out what you put in. Simply creating an account and posting content isn't likely to lead to success in the cluttered social media landscape.

Most social networks can be used to add value for almost any marketing strategy or for any business. The key to success is to determine which social networks are most suited to your marketing objectives.

For example, businesses use Facebook to build awareness by creating a Page, to drive conversions by using retargeting ads, or to gain leads by promoting content or through lead ads. Facebook can be used for almost any marketing objective, but it will be used differently based on the goal.

For most social networks there are three broad approaches that businesses use to drive impact:

Organic Approach
An organic approach to social media means that the business wants to use social media to connect with people in a relevant way – without running ads as the primary goal.

While some say that organic reach is dead, they are usually referring to Facebook, and even on Facebook there are many businesses that generate significant organic reach by sharing great content and keeping their community engaged.

This can be a challenging approach for businesses as it takes significant time and effort to successfully break through the clutter and create content that people want. If you can achieve this, the payout can be huge.

Brands relying on this strategy focus on creating great content and interacting with people to build connections and community on the social network.

 Example:
We recently ran a content workshop with an organization on Facebook that was seeing 1% organic reach. After improving their content and creating more interesting videos their organic reach now averages 10% of their fans, and they generate tens of thousands of views of their best content.

Paid Approach
As organic reach has become more challenging, many businesses find that they aren't able to create content that breaks-through the noise and also promotes their business, so they focus their efforts on a paid approach to social media by running ads.

Rather than focusing on gaining organic exposure it is easier for many businesses to use social media as a paid advertising channel. Social networks have huge audiences and tremendous targeting opportunities making them cost-effective ways to advertise online.

Most businesses now have paid social media as a part of their strategy. Since their posts will organically only reach a small percentage of their fans, boosting posts or advertising is a key way to use the network to get your message in front of people without the challenges of gaining an organic following.

Big Idea:
Even if you are using a paid approach to social media, you still need great content. Ads that aren't of value to people generally cost more and have lower impact.

Community Approach
A community approach to social media is where a business has a strategy to empower others to create, post, and share content instead of creating all of the content themselves.

With the rise of Instagram Influencers, more and more businesses are using others to spread their message. This strategy isn't only for influencers though. Many businesses use hashtags, incentives, and even just suggestions to get people talking on social media.

Big Idea:
For many businesses word-of-mouth is one of the top drivers of sales, yet few businesses employ a strategy to get people talking. Think about the naturally

"talkable" parts of your business experience and inspire or incentivize people to share.

Using the trust that social media users have in the people they follow and encouraging them to share their stories on social media is a big missed opportunity for many businesses.

When I bought a new car, I was really excited about it, and I shared pictures on social media. I didn't, however, mention the car dealership. This would have been a good opportunity for the dealership to gain exposure on social media. They could give me a hashtag to use or ask that I tag their account. If they offer me an incentive, even better.

Many businesses are so focused on their own content that they forget the power of encouraging others to share on social media as well.

This is often easier and more effective than creating your own presence and following.

Remember:
Keep in mind that most businesses don't exclusively use one approach on all social networks or even on one. You may use a hybrid of the approaches above, however it's worth considering the resources you have available as it can be challenging and require more time and money to effectively execute all three strategies.

Stages to Building Your Presence

When it comes to building your social media presence there are four steps that you should plan for each social network: Profile, People, Post, and Participate.

Big Idea:
As you build your social presence, be sure you plan for each of these stages to maximize your chances of success. Many businesses only focus on Profile and Post and don't sufficiently build an audience for their profiles.

Step 1: Profile
Build a solid profile is the first step. As you build your profile consider best practices for the platform.

A few tips for building a strong social media profile:
- Use a consistent username on every platform
- Create a square and circle version of your logo for your profile image on social networks (most require square and circle)
- Make sure images are the right size
- Use appealing language that will inspire someone to connect with you
- Write a clear and compelling "about" or "bio" section that explains what you do and who should follow you

Step 2: People
Once you have a profile the next step is to get people to follow you! There are many strategies and tactics that you can use to build a following, and what works is a little different on each platform. What isn't different is that you need a clear and compelling value proposition and great content to really connect with people.

Big Idea:
At this stage it is also helpful to consider your overall strategy and value proposition for the network, as you may want to incorporate this into your profile description. Ask yourself: why should someone follow me here? What will they get out of it?

Build a plan to attract followers to your account. Beyond posting regular, compelling content, some of the most popular strategies are:

- Ads
- Email
- Community building
- Like and follow other accounts
- In-store signage
- On-site or in-store
- Contests or promotions
- In-person events
- Employees

Step 3: Post

Posting regular content that people love is important to maintain your presence and drive business impact. Each network has different norms in terms of frequency. It is important to consider how often you have great content and build your calendar around the content you have vs. an arbitrary schedule.

Tool: Scheduling
There are many tools that will allow you to schedule social media posts in advance. Most networks now allow you to create scheduled posts, but you can also use tools like Buffer or Sprout Social to schedule posts to multiple networks.

As you consider your content plan, it may be helpful to think upfront about the assets that you will need to execute. Don't be afraid to experiment with different kinds of content – especially when you are starting out.

Big Idea:
Be sure to regularly analyze your content so you know what works and doesn't. Content trends change over time and staying aware of how your

content is performing as well as experimentation will future-proof your content strategy.

Step 4: Participate

Participating on social media is important – it is called *social* media for a reason. Different networks allow for different levels of interaction between business accounts and people.

For all networks you should plan to:
- Monitor and respond to comments
- Like posts or comments mentioning you
- Like other Pages when possible
- Tag other accounts
- Use hashtags as appropriate

For networks that allow businesses to connect with other people, you should plan to:
- Follow other accounts
- Like and comment on posts
- Share posts from others

Some large and well-loved brands are able to build a following just by being present, however most businesses have to work at connecting with others to build their presence.

Tool: Management
There are many social media management tools that make it easy to find and connect with others, as well as respond to comments. Hootsuite and Sprout Social are popular for this for smaller businesses, and Sprinklr is one of the more popular enterprise tools.

Social Network Best Practices

Social media best practices are different for each network. Below you'll find a summary image that shows the best practices for each social network from an implementation standpoint.

A few best practices to keep in mind that apply to all social networks.

- **Look, learn, and listen first** – When getting started most businesses start by posting right away. Start by listening and looking. See what content performs well. Listen to how others are interacting. Build off of the successful strategies that you can observe before creating your own content.
- **Content over calendars** – Focus on posting when you have good, relevant content for your target audience. This is more important than a schedule.
- **Content matters most** – If you don't have great content it doesn't matter what time of day you post. Focus on creating content that drives impact. Most social networks give you access to analytics, so you can see what is performing.
- **Don't be spammy** – Many social networks allow you to connect with other people and send them individual messages or tag them. Don't send private mass-messages to people – they find it annoying and you can get blocked from some networks for doing this.
- **Consistent posting** – Don't expect results overnight, and make sure that you are consistent in your execution. It sometimes takes time to build an audience and get results.
- **Reply, engage, and connect** – Each network is different in terms of how businesses can interact with people, but social media should be social. Engage and interact with the people you want to reach in order to get noticed and build your following.

- **Analytics are your best friend** – Take time to review your analytics regularly so you know what is and isn't working. Many businesses don't get results because they continue to deploy a strategy that isn't generating results. Pay attention and make changes as needed.
- **Consistent presence** – Make sure that you setup a consistent presence on all social networks so that you are building a strong branded presence for your business.

Power Tip:
Reserve your username on EVERY social network (including those you don't plan on using immediately) so that you can build a consistent presence if you choose to add the network later.

Tool: NameVine
Go to namevine.com to see if your desired username is available. It will check the major platforms all in one search and easily allow you to consider alternatives if it is not.

Best practices in terms of content, types of posts, and frequency are usually different for each social network. The chart below shows best practices at a glance for the most popular platforms.

Following these should be your starting point, but you may find that different things work better for your specific audience.

Digital Marketing That Actually Works

	Facebook	Instagram	Twitter	YouTube	LinkedIn	Pinterest	Snapchat
POSTING FREQUENCY	**1-4x** per week	**1-7x** per week	**2-10x** per day, including retweets & replies	Weekly or when applicable	**1-7x** per week	**3-14x** per week	**4-7x** per week
WHEN TO POST	When relevant to audience	When audience is online	Spread throughout the day	When audience is online	During business hours	Spread throughout the day	When relevant to audience
USE OF HASHTAGS	Limited search functionality. Recommended: **1-2** per post	Recommended: **20-30** per post	Recommended: **1-2** per tweet	Use in descriptions. Recommended: **a handful** per upload	Recommended: **1-5** per post	Recommended: **3-5** per post	Not popularly used
BEST PERFORMING CONTENT	Photos • Videos	Photos • Short videos	Questions • Multimedia	Product Reviews • How-to Guides • Educational videos	News • Updates • Articles	Style • Home • Food & Drink • Beauty	Fun & playful • Lenses & filters
IDEAL VIDEO LENGTH	**1 Minute** for video **5+ Mins** for Live video	**30 Seconds**	**45 Seconds**	**2 Minutes**	**1-2 Minutes**	Based on source video	**10 Seconds**
CONTENT TIPS	Thumb-stopping power • Short & catchy videos & images • Respond to comments	Real photos of real things • Use hashtags • Single focus of image	Mix content • Retweet • Reply and participate	Clear purpose for video • Compelling storyline • Add variety to video topics	Positive & relevant content • Add images & video • Value for audience	Variety of content • Create multiple boards • Curate content from other sources	Capture attention • Showcase business or product • Fun & light
AUDIENCE BUILDING TIPS	Post Consistent and engaging content • Boost posts	Use hashtags • Engage with audience	Tweet more often • Use hashtags and participate	Optimize for search • Post consistently	Add contacts to your network • Engage via comments and groups	Post often • Create searchable descriptions	User-generated content • Cross-promote on other platforms

Want to see the full size image online? Go to www.ThatActuallyWorks.com/DigitalMarketing and download the *Digital Marketing that Actually Works Bonuses* to get a high-res image.

Social Media: Choosing Where to Play

There are many social networks and choosing where to play can be a challenge. There is no single answer for where businesses should start.

When choosing which social networks to participate in, consider the following factors:

PEOPLE
Be where your audience is.

- Is your audience there?
- Are they engaged?

NETWORK
Invest energy in the networks that are best set-up to help you achieve your business objectives. For example, Instagram doesn't allow users to share links, so it usually isn't an ideal network for businesses wanting to drive leads or sales directly.

- How does the network let users participate?
- How do people use the network and are they open to your message?

RETURN
What do you hope to realistically get out of participating in the network? If you are new to social media you may not know, but it can be helpful to research benchmarks and set some goals and expectations. Many businesses jump into a network with no idea of what they are hoping to achieve and eventually find that their efforts didn't drive the results they wanted.

- What is your estimated impact/result?

INVESTMENT

How much time, effort, and resources will your execution take? Some networks may be less resource-intensive to build a presence on. Be sure you understand what you need to invest and compare this to your anticipated return to make sure you are maximizing your return on investment (ROI).

- What is the estimated cost/time/effort to succeed?
- Consider time, tools, growing your following, etc.

Remember:
It is better to do one network well vs. many poorly. Focus on gaining success with one network before you add another. Many businesses find that focused efforts on a single network or two gives them significant business results.

Social Media Marketing

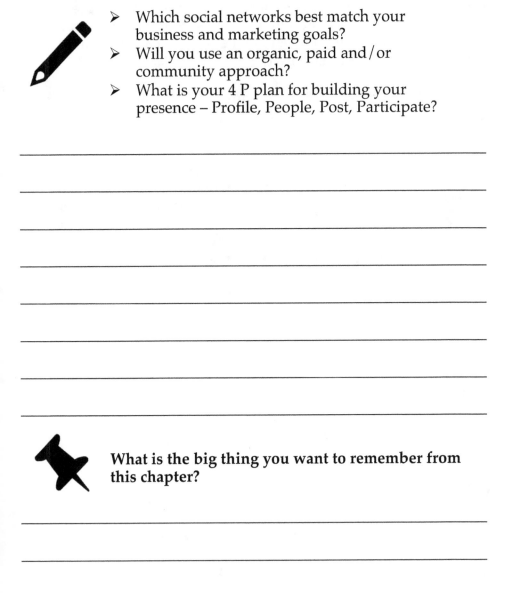

- ➤ Which social networks best match your business and marketing goals?
- ➤ Will you use an organic, paid and/or community approach?
- ➤ What is your 4 P plan for building your presence – Profile, People, Post, Participate?

What is the big thing you want to remember from this chapter?

Go to www.ThatActuallyWorks.com/DigitalMarketing for your free action planner and bonus resources.

Chapter 7: Digital Advertising

Digital advertising is estimated at over 50% of advertising budgets. Plus, digital advertising offers unprecedented flexibility and transparency.

Any business can get started on any budget. The results are instantly available so if something isn't working you can pause and regroup. If something is working you can do more of it.

There are also many more digital advertising options available than ever before, so businesses have a huge opportunity to reach their target audience in a relevant, cost-effective way.

Types of Digital Ads

In this book we will focus on the four primary types of digital ads: Search, Social, Video, and Display. There is a section on affiliate advertising at the end of this chapter, as it works differently vs. the other types of ads.

Within each type of ad (for example within Social Ads) there may be multiple ad formats. An ad format is the way the ad is displayed. For example, on Facebook you can choose a video ad, an image ad, a lead ad, or a collection ad, which allows users to click through multiple products, for example.

Below are some of the ad formats available in Facebook.

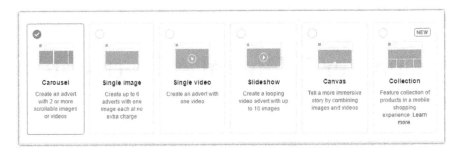

All of the advertising formats discussed below offer self-serve platforms, which means that anyone can login and easily place an ad. Most ad platforms allow you to get started for as little as a few dollars.

A word of caution: If you aren't familiar with an ad platform take the time to learn about it before placing an ad. Many marketers have made small mistakes in their ad setup that has cost them thousands of dollars. Be careful about how you set your budgets and monitor your spending closely.

Power Tip:
Start small, test, and learn. The advantage of digital advertising is that you don't have to commit to a large budget upfront. Spend some time exploring and figuring out what works. Once you have that information you can increase your budget.

Search Ads

Search ads are the ads that appear around search engine results. You can choose to have your ad appear when someone searches for a specific term. Google is the largest search network, followed by Bing.

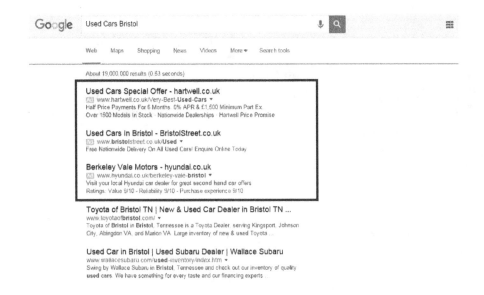

Search ads are popular for businesses because you can find people who are looking for your product or service right now.

How they are purchased:
With search ads, businesses pay per click, so you only pay when someone clicks on your ads. The amount you pay is based on a bidding system, or, in other words, the demand from other advertisers as well as the volume of people searching. Some search terms can cost as little as a few cents up to over $20 per click.

Business Objectives
Search ads are popular because you are able to find people who are specifically looking for your product or something related to your product.

Search ads work best if you have a product or service that people search for with intention to choose or buy. For example, search ads are great for a video production company, as people often search for providers to get videos made. Search ads work well for both B2B and B2C businesses.

Search ads don't work well for products or services that people don't specifically search for. For example, we worked with a company called Project Blue Collar that aims to raise awareness for Rescue Dogs. They aren't a rescue shelter and don't take-in rescue dogs. They weren't able to find search terms that were likely to send relevant traffic to their site.

When They Don't Work:
Search ads don't work with very low dollar purchase items and can be challenging in highly competitive industries.

With low dollar value purchases it is often difficult for the economics of search ads to work. For example, if you sell a $5 product and pay $1/click, 1 in every 5 visitors will have to buy from you just to break EVEN on revenue. If your profit margin is 50% you would need 1 in every 2.5 visitors to buy. It can be challenging to make the economics work.

Search ads can also be tricky in very competitive industries with well-established players. For example, most ecommerce products will compete against Amazon, eBay, and other large retailers. These retailers have well-designed search campaigns and can often pay more per click since users buy a variety of products on their site once they click.

Targeting:
Search ads are targeted by keyword, meaning you target the ad to show when people search for specific words or phrases.

The key to success is to choose keywords that send highly qualified visitors to your site. Search ads should be regularly optimized to be sure that the most effective keywords are getting most of the budget.

You can also choose to only run your ads in specific geographic areas.

Formats:
Since search ads are text-only, they are relatively easy to create and implement.

Tool: Google Keyword Planner
If you are curious to know how many searches there are for your business or industry the Google Keyword Planner tool shows search volume for search terms and the estimated cost per click to run ads for a search term. You need a Google Ads account to access the keyword tool, but it is free to use. It can be found at **ads.google.com** under "tools".

Social Ads

Social media ads are ads that appear on social networks. Most established social networks (Facebook, Twitter, Instagram, LinkedIn, Pinterest, Snapchat) have well-established self-service advertising platforms.

Social media ads are popular because they are inexpensive and have very focused targeting opportunities. Businesses can target their ads to find exactly who they want to reach.

How they are purchased:
Most social ads are purchased based on a bidding system, which means that the more people who want to reach the target audience you selected, the more expensive it will be.

When it comes to what you pay for, you can pay for social ads based on an impression (when someone sees your ad), for reach (number of people who see your ad), for clicks (people who click on your ad), leads (people who submit a lead form), and more. Based on your advertising objective you'll have relevant choices of what you want to pay for.

Business Objectives:
Social ads are good for almost any business objective because there are so many different targeting options, formats, and buying types. The key to success is to choose the most relevant business objective for your target audience.

When They Don't Work:
From a business standpoint, since there are so many types of social ads they work for most businesses in more scenarios. Social ads often don't work when they aren't set-up well or when the content isn't impactful for the audience.

Targeting:
Social ads offer some of the most appealing targeting options online. Since social networks know so much about their users they are able to offer incredibly robust targeting options for advertisers.

Social ads allow targeting based on a broad range of demographics, interests, and behaviors. Below are some of the targeting options available in Facebook ads.

- Location – include and exclude down to the zip code level
- Demographics – basic age, gender, etc.
- Advanced demographics – marital status, education, income, parents, etc.

- Interests – topics, categories or even pages that people have expressed an interest in
- Behaviors – things that people do online like shopping, making donations, in the market for a vehicle etc. (these vary by country)

Power Tip:
Facebook has very robust interest targeting and detailed demographics. You can create a Facebook Ad account for free and explore the targeting options to get an idea for just how detailed your targeting can be.

In addition to the general targeting options above, social networks usually allow businesses to target custom audiences that are built based on people that they have already interacted with.

- Website retargeting – You can retarget people who have visited your website. This can be targeted to the site overall, specific pages, or groups of pages.
- List retargeting – You can also upload email and phone lists and retarget people based on this information. The ad platform will match the email address or phone number with a profile on their site and serve your ads to those people. Most good lists have a match rate from 60 - 80%.
- People who interacted with you – You can usually also target ads to people who like your Page or people who have interacted with content on your Page.
- Look-a-like audiences – Look-a-like audiences are created based off of a custom audience. The ad network will aim to find people who have similar characteristics to the audience that you created. For example, I can create a look-a-like audience of my website visitors, and Facebook will analyze my website visitors and create a new target audience of people who are similar. Many businesses get good results with look-a-like audiences since the algorithm-based

analysis can be more effective at finding ideal customers vs. manual targeting.

Power Tip:
In order to use website retargeting you have to add some code to your website called a pixel. This is something that can be executed easily by your web developer and allows Facebook to connect information from your site to Facebook. If you are in Europe or your website has visitors in the EU you will need to make sure you are GDPR compliant.

Other social networks like LinkedIn, Twitter, and Pinterest have similar targeting options available.

Formats:
There are many ad formats available on social networks, and new ones are added regularly. Most ads will include an image or a video to maximize visual impact.

Prior to launching a social media ad, review the ad formats available on the network and choose the one that best matches your business objectives and creative idea.

Video Ads

While social media and display ads can have video as a format, when we talk about video ads as a channel we are discussing ads that appear before, during, or after a video online.

These are usually on YouTube, but can also be on other networks, like online streaming services, such as Hulu.

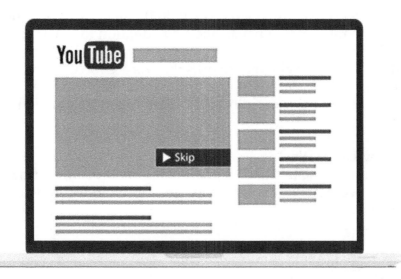

How they are purchased:
Video ads are generally purchased based on impressions or views.
An impression means that someone was served your ad – even for
a fraction of a second. A view refers to the ad being viewed for a
specific amount of time. Each ad network defines a video view
differently.

When ads are force-viewed, meaning they appear before or during
content you may purchase different lengths of views – for example
a 6 second view or a 15 second view.
The amount you pay for your ad is based on an open bidding
system based on supply and demand.

Business Objectives:
Video ads are best at top-of-funnel ad objectives like brand
awareness/attract and equity/nurture.

While you can run video ads on Facebook and Display, the view
times on these mediums tend to be extremely short. Some Facebook
videos have average watch times of only 1 second. This is because

social media and display video ads run in the news feed or content – meaning people have to pause and pay attention to have impact.

On YouTube or other video networks the ads are forced view because they appear within the content. This means that they can have a bigger impact; especially since video is a more impactful medium.

When They Don't Work:
If you don't have the budget for great video creative this format won't work well. Generally video ads are a good fit for mid-sized to large businesses.

Unlike social networks, where a wide variety of videos can work on YouTube your ad is shown more like a commercial, so you'll want to have creative that is designed for the format.

Video ads are great for top-of-funnel marketing objectives like attract and nurture, but usually aren't great at achieving action. Not a lot of people click on video ads, so they aren't good at driving purchases.

Targeting:
Video ads can be targeted a few different ways depending on the network. On YouTube, ads can be targeted by demographics or on the content you want the video to appear alongside.

Formats:
Formats for video ads are typically based on the length of the ad (6 seconds, 15 seconds, etc.) and whether or not the ad is skippable.

Display Ads

Display ads are ads that appear around content online. For example, if you are reading a news site and see ads around the content, those would be display ads.

Display ads are purchased through ad networks and Google is one of the most popular ad networks.

How they are purchased:
Display ads are typically purchased per impression (when someone is served your ad), per viewable impression (when someone is served your ad and sees it for a set amount of time), or per click.

Display ads are sold based on a bidding system, so the actual price you pay is based on the supply and demand for the target audience that you want to reach.

Business Objectives:
Display ads can work for a variety of business objectives. They are most effective at building awareness since they typically appear around content.

If you choose to pay per click, display ads can be effective at driving traffic or conversions to your website.

When They Don't Work:
Display ads may not be effective at equity or nurture type of objectives that require a more complex message or a more impactful impression.

Most display ads are viewed passively – they are around the content that someone is looking at. This means that people are not typically spending a lot of time viewing them.

If your message is complex or you want to build specific brand equity, a more impactful format like video usually produces better results.

Targeting:
Display ad targeting is based on information that the ad server (for example Google) has about the audience, as well as the content that the ad appears on or around.

- Demographics – Ads can be targeted based on the demographics of the viewer.
- Interests and affinity – Ads can be purchased based on interests that people have or areas that they show an affinity for.
- In-market – Ads can be targeted at people who are in the market or actively shopping for something specific.
- Content – Ads can be targeted based on the content that they appear on or around. You can target by a specific website or the subject area of the website – for example fitness sites – or the content of the article – for example a fitness article on the New York Times.

Power Tip:
Content targeting can make sure that your audience is interested in or receptive to your ad. For example, I may be interested in fitness but if I'm reading a finance post, it isn't relevant at that point in time. By targeting content, you can be sure your audience in the right place at the right to time to take in your ad.

An ad can use multiple sets of these targeting choices at once -for example women between 30 and 50 who are interested in fitness and visiting a fitness website.

Formats:
Display ads can take on a wide variety of formats, and the Interactive Advertising Bureau, or IAB has created standards to ensure that ad formats are consistent across publishers.

Generally, display ads are images, rotating images, or videos and they can be created to be interactive and clickable.

Choosing Ad Channels

Each ad channel has pros and cons and is appropriate for different business objectives. Many established advertisers will run ads on one or more channels.

If you are starting out, choose the one channel that is most likely to get you results and focus on that first.

Below is a "Cheat Sheet" of digital advertising channels sorted by the business objectives that they are usually most effective at.

Channel	Awareness	Nurture	Convert	Retain/ Advocacy
Display/ Programmatic	Inexpensive reach	Views may be more passive, less involved	Typically low click rates	Inexpensive reach with retargeting options
Search ads	More expensive per click for top-of-funnel awareness	Connect with interested in category	Connect with motivated searchers	Expensive way to reconnect with customers
YouTube	Longer video views (6 second bumpers inexpensive)	Longer video views (True-view ads)	Few people click	Depends on objective
Facebook	Inexpensive reach (although short view times)	Need thumb-stopping content to drive longer views	Efficient conversions with right call to action	Retargeting and broad reach
Instagram	Inexpensive reach (although short view times)	Stories can drive longer view times	Instagrammers less likely to change tasks	Retargeting and broad reach

To download a full cheat sheet, go to www.ThatActuallyWorks.com/DigitalMarketing and a high-resolution image will be included in the downloads.

Trends in Digital Advertising

Digital advertising is still an evolving aspect of digital marketing. While it isn't new any more, industry norms, guidelines, and best practices are still emerging.

The IAB (iab.com) is the industry standard for digital advertising and they set guidelines for advertisers and publishers to create more harmony in the digital advertising industry.

Programmatic

Programmatic advertising refers to the automation of digital advertising. With programmatic advertising ad suppliers, or publishers who have advertising inventory are automatically matched with advertisers, or buyers of ads instantly.

Prior to the rise of programmatic advertising, most ads were purchased based on negotiations for a set price. For example, a baby brand may choose to advertise on BabyCenter.com for a set price.

With programmatic the process is automated, which allows advertisers to maximize the impact that they generate from their ad budget. For example, an advertiser wanting to target baby content can now automatically run ads on thousands of baby sites for the best price possible.

Facebook and Google ads are purchased programmatically, as are ads purchased through most online ad platforms.

Ad Fraud and Viewability

Ad fraud and viewability are popular topics in digital advertising circles, and they highlight some of the challenges that advertisers have with digital.

Ad Fraud is primarily an issue in display advertising, as ads appear all over the Internet on different platforms without a lot of control. Ad fraud essentially happens when publishers create false impressions in order to generate revenue from advertisers. So, advertisers are paying for ads that people didn't actually see.

Over the years, much ad fraud has been detected and advertising platforms have more controls in place to minimize this. That being said, there are still issues where millions of ad dollars are spent on false impressions.

Ad Viewability is when advertisers want to make sure that their ad was in view by a human for a reasonable amount of time (usually a few seconds). This issue has plagued digital advertising since the beginning.

The challenge is that just because an ad loads on a page doesn't mean that the requirements have been met. Ad platforms have started to crack down on this more and more, offering only viewable impressions as inventory, but with so many different sites and placements it is difficult to monitor.

These issues are mostly limited to display ads, since search, social, and video ads happen on more controlled platforms. Most advertisers with small spending (in the tens of thousands or less) won't need to focus on these issues. Bigger advertisers who invest heavily in display often use software and third-party tools to monitor and mitigate ad fraud and viewability issues.

Brand Safety

Brand safety has emerged as an issue as businesses want to understand what content their ad appears around. In television we often hear about advertisers "pulling" their ads from shows that are offensive.

Online advertisers want the same amount of control about where their ads show up. With many advertising channels like Facebook and YouTube relying on user-generated content, it is difficult for businesses to control where their ads are displayed.

Advertisers have been horrified to find that their ads are displayed on a video promoting white supremacy for example.

This tends to be an issue more relevant for big brands, and ad platforms have adopted technologies and controls to minimize this risk. Advertisers can have more control over where their content displays if they are concerned about this.

Down-Funnel Ad Objectives

As we look at how digital advertising platforms are evolving, one of the things that we are seeing is that there is more focus on tracking and optimizing for on-site behavior and conversions.

Meaning, instead of running ads where you pay for and optimize for clicks, you can now run ads where you pay for and optimize for on-site sales or email signups. Advertising platforms are using algorithms and on-site tracking to find the people who are most likely to convert and are targeting ads at them.

This allows businesses that have online stores or lead-funnels to take their targeting to get better results from their ad spending. As advertisers track more and more online behavior (which may be alarming) it means that they can also better target ads and make your ad spend even more efficient.

Personalization and Customization

Personalization and customization are emerging as opportunities for marketers to run more effective ads. The idea is to create ads that are customized or personalized to the specific person seeing them.

For example, a business selling custom cakes could create one ad targeting women who are planning a wedding and another targeting moms who are planning children's birthday parties. Even though the product is the same, the ads can be targeted differently for different audiences.

In the example below, you can see how a restaurant can choose different targeting based on their objectives.

| Targeting Young People | Targeting Older Folks |

Decide who your target audience is before you design your ad. It may affect the image and the way you write copy. How old are they? 18-25? 25-54? Where do they live? Anywhere? In Boise, Idaho? What kinds of things are they interested in? Family Activities? College sports? For more information on targeting options, click here.

Mobile Surpasses Desktop

While this arguably isn't new or a trend, many businesses have not yet adapted their strategy to one of mobile first. Mobile is over twice the size of desktop and is projected to continue to grow quickly.

This should not be surprising as time spent on mobile devices is growing dramatically. What this means is that you need to make sure that every aspect of your digital advertising strategy – from the ads to your website experience – is not just optimized for mobile but made for mobile first.

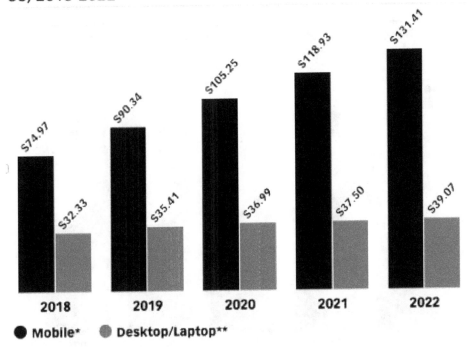

Digital Ad Spending, by Device

US, 2018-2022

Bars (Mobile*): $74.97 (2018), $90.34 (2019), $105.25 (2020), $118.93 (2021), $131.41 (2022)

Bars (Desktop/Laptop**): $32.33 (2018), $35.41 (2019), $36.99 (2020), $37.50 (2021), $39.07 (2022)

● Mobile*   ● Desktop/Laptop**

Emergence of Big Players

When it comes to digital ads, Facebook and Google are by far the biggest players in the space. Google accounts for about 40% of digital ad revenue and Facebook accounts for around 20%.

While Google represents significantly more market share vs. Facebook, the Google ads are run on three distinct platforms: YouTube, Display, and Search.

With these players making up so much of digital ad spending, most businesses focus their efforts on them and replicate on others as appropriate. For example, Google Search ads can be uploaded into Bing Search Ads to automatically replicate the strategy.

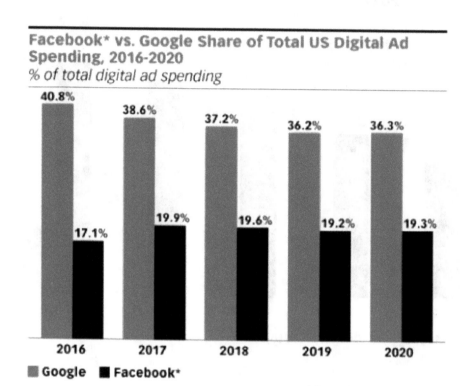

Facebook* vs. Google Share of Total US Digital Ad Spending, 2016-2020
% of total digital ad spending

Driving Impact in Digital Advertising

When it comes to driving impact in digital advertising it's helpful to think about the "levers" involved in executing a digital advertising campaign.

When driving impact, there are a number of elements to consider.

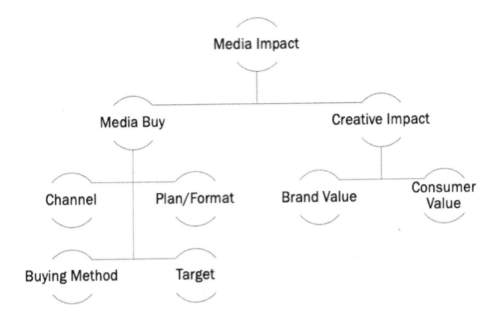

Media Buying

The first side of the equation is the media buying choices. Media buying focuses on where your ads are displayed and how they are purchased.

Channel
The first decision is the channel where your ads will be displayed. By "channel" consider if Search, Social, Display, or Video is most likely to achieve your objectives.
Because creating and optimizing ads for a channel will take time and effort, it's best to choose one channel and maximize it before adding new channels.

Buying Method and Budget
Once you've selected your channel, the next decision is the buying method and budget. The buying method will be largely dictated by your business objectives.

Buying method refers to what you are paying for with your digital ads. For example, you may pay for clicks, impressions, website visits, or even conversions.

You also need to decide what your budget is and how you want to allocate it. Some businesses run "always on" campaigns that constantly run and are optimized in real time. Other businesses operate in more campaign style where they spend set budgets on specific communications objectives.

Plan/Format
The plan or format refers to the decision of the ad format as well as the overall creative plan.

From an ad format standpoint you'll have to choose the one that best achieves your business objectives and that is right for your creative. This could be video, image, carousel, etc.

Once you know the format of the ads and your budget, you can determine how to plan or split the budget across your campaigns or creatives. Depending on your approach to digital advertising, there are different ways to do this.

Some businesses build their digital plan based on trial + optimization. They have a budget in mind for the year and try different things and push the budget towards what works best. This agile approach works well for small to medium businesses who are actively managing campaigns and want to get the most out of their efforts.

Larger businesses that do media plans will create a plan in advance around how they want to break up their budget. Even if you have a media plan in place, to maximize your results you should allow for flexibility to react to them and pause underperforming campaigns or increase budgets on ads that perform well.

Target Audience
The target audience is who you want to see your ad. Each channel has different targeting options, and you can get very specific and focused in who you choose to target.

As you consider your targeting options it's important that it is neither too broad nor too specific. The size of your target audience is also largely determined by your budget. If you have $100 to spend on an ad your target should be smaller than if you have $100,000 to spend.

A good rule of thumb for ad targeting is to aim to reach 50% of the target audience with your ad.

When you define your target audience, the ad platform will show you how big your audience is. For example, if I want to reach women 30 – 50 who love coffee and live in Cincinnati, Facebook may have 100,000 people who match that description.

When I enter my budget, Facebook will give me an estimate of how many people I can reach. For example, if I spend $100 I can reach 10,000 people. In this case I would only be reaching 10% of the target audience. I may want to try to be more specific on who I really want to reach with additional demographic or interest targeting to make my ad as impactful as possible.

Power Tip:
In general, the more targeted your audience is the more expensive they will be to reach. This is because of the supply and demand nature of the bidding system – the smaller the audience the lower the supply. This isn't necessarily an issue, as you will be reaching an audience that is more receptive to your product or service, so your ultimate business impact should be good.

Creative Impact

In addition to the mechanics of media buying, channels, and targeting, creating actual creative ads that have the desired impact is also important.

To maximize your ad effectiveness, you should aim to have both brand value and user value.

Brand Value
Brand value means that the creative is constructed to achieve your business objective. It is important that your brand is immediately present in the creative (especially video) and that the ad is crafted to deliver on your business objective.

User Value
User value means that the ad is interesting to the target audience. Almost all advertising networks evaluate this and offer a "score" as to how relevant your ad is. Facebook provides a relevance score and Google has a quality score.

User value is important for two main reasons.

First, your ad cost will decrease if people are interested in your ad. Most bidding formulas include user value in their equation, meaning that the price you pay for an ad is a combination of the market competitiveness through bidding and the user value. On Facebook for example I've seen businesses reduce their costs by over 50% just by creating better creative.

User value is also important because if people find your ad interesting and dwell on it, it will have more impact. For example, if your ad is boring and I quickly scroll by, it hasn't had much of an impact on me. On the other had if your ad catches my attention and I pause to look at it or interact with it, it has more value to your business.

Effective Digital Advertising – OCTO

The biggest key to success in your digital advertising is to tightly and effectively match your objective, content, and target, and then to optimize, which we refer to as OCTO.

Many ad campaigns are not effective because one or more of these elements is poorly defined or executed.

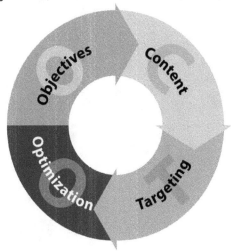

Objective

The first step is to clearly define the objective of your ad. Each ad can have only one objective, so it is important that you choose wisely.

The ad objective is what you want the ad to achieve for you. Compared to traditional advertising, digital ads are much more detailed in the objectives that they can achieve. Many traditional marketers are used to incorporating multiple objectives into a single ad "We want to build awareness and drive people to the website." In digital you have to choose one objective to optimize for.

Choosing the right ad objective is important because once that decision has been made, the other parts of the ad will be pre-defined based on it. For example, if your objective is clicks, you will pay per click for the ad. The ad will then be delivered to the people who are most likely to click on it.

Each ad network provides slightly different choices for ad objectives and they frequently add new ones. As you can see in the example of Facebook ad objectives below, there are many objectives that can be selected, even for a single marketing objective.

What's your marketing objective?

Awareness	Consideration	Conversion
Brand awareness	Traffic	Conversions
Reach	Engagement	Product catalog sales
	App installs	Store visits
	Video views	
	Lead generation	
	Messages	

Each ad objective may also have different creative. For example, the creative that you would use to generate clicks would be different than the creative aimed at building awareness.

Building creative that specifically matches your business objective will give you the best probability of success.

| Drive Foot Traffic | Sell A Product | Brand Awareness |

Start by deciding what your ad is intended to do. Are you trying to push a certain product? Drive foot traffic to your store? Encourage website views? Improve trust? Identifying the purpose of your advertising will help you build posts that deliver the desired results.

Targeting

Once your ad objective is selected you can choose your target audience. Many businesses don't take full advantage of the targeting options available.

Define your audience as specifically as possible, and don't be afraid to create multiple ads aimed at multiple target audiences. You can segment your audience into smaller targets in order to reach each one effectively.

For example, if I am a restaurant and I want to reach people 20 – 50, I can segment them into groups: 20 – 30, 30 – 40 and 40 -50 and send different ads to each one. I am still reaching the same broad audience, but by segmenting, each audience can receive an ad that is best tailored to them.

Depending on your business and your objective this may be more effective than trying to reach everyone with the same creative.

Targeting Young People   **Targeting Older Folks**

Decide who your target audience is before you design your ad. It may affect the image and the way you write copy. How old are they? 18-25? 25-54? Where do they live? Anywhere? In Boise, Idaho? What kinds of things are they interested in? Family Activities? College sports? For more information on targeting options, click here.

Content

Great content or creative is the key to success in digital ads. Businesses sometimes get so lost in the technical elements of running ads that they forget about the creative, or don't put as much thought into it as needed.

We touched on creative in the previous sections on objectives and targeting to highlight that these choices could and should result in different creative.

Creative should be created to achieve your business objective and be as relevant as possible to your target audience. In addition, you'll want to incorporate best practices to give your content the best chance possible of standing out.

Power Tip:
The biggest thing that you can do for your content is to keep it simple and focused. Most people spend only a fraction of a second on your content initially, so clean and compelling visuals or videos with a single message are most likely to stand out.

What motivates your customer?   Address their concerns (like prices).   Entertain them.

Consider talking about things in terms of your customer's mindset and what might appeal to them emotionally. While you spend a lot of time thinking about your business, customers spend most of their time thinking about their own lives. So put yourself in their shoes and think "what would make me like this business?"

Power Tip:
If you want to know if your content is standing out, look at your quality score or relevance score. In as little as 500 impressions, an ad network can tell you if your ad is relevant to the audience that you are sending it to.

Digital ad platforms are also setup to allow for automatic testing and optimization of content. For example, you can upload a number of different creatives, and the ad platform will quickly determine which ad is generating the best results and put the ad budget towards that ad.

Therefore, it's always a good idea to have multiple creative variants to maximize your budget toward the best performing ad.

Power Tip:
Most ad platforms allow you to upload multiple creatives and will automatically optimize. In addition, they allow you to run A/B split tests where you can test elements of your creative to determine what performs best.

Optimize

Optimizing your digital ads is vital to your success and is one of the things that make digital ads such a powerful marketing tool.

Once you have created and started running your ad, you aren't locked into anything. You can still make changes to any element of your ad based on how it's performing. Many businesses do the work upfront to create a great ad, but then let the ad run without checking in on it.

There is a famous saying in marketing – "I know half of my ad spend is wasted, I just don't know which half."

Not anymore.

We can know if we take the time.

Even with the best planning and the best creative minds, we don't always know how something will work until we put it out there. Digital ads should be regularly optimized and updated based on real-time performance.

When getting started you'll want to check in regularly, maybe daily, to see how things are performing and make changes. As you gain experience and once you've done some initial optimizations you may check in and optimize weekly.

Big Idea:
If you have an agency running your ads, ask them what their optimization plan is. Make sure that they are checking your ads regularly and optimizing your budget to maximize your return on investment.

Digital Advertising

> ➤ How can you use Search, Social, Video and display ads for your business goals? Which is most important and why?
> ➤ What is your OCTO strategy to execute your ads: Objective, Content, Target and Optimization plan?

_____

_____

_____

_____

_____

_____

_____

What is the big thing you want to remember from this chapter?

_____

_____

Go to www.ThatActuallyWorks.com/DigitalMarketing for your free action planner and bonus resources.

Chapter 8: SEO (Search Engine Optimization)

Search Engine Optimization or SEO is about optimizing your website with the aim of having it show up towards the top of organic search engine results.

On a search engine results page, about 80% of users click on the organic (non-paid) search results and the top three rankings get most of the clicks.

Google is by far the biggest search engine, so we'll use Google as the example, and the principles of what works for Google generally works for other search engines as well.

SEO is a key strategy for most businesses because if your site is well optimized for search engines you can have a steady flow of highly qualified people visiting your site regularly.

SEO brings business results:
- 60-80% of traffic from search
- Generates traffic + revenue

If you want these results from your website, you need SEO, because "Build It and They Will Come" only works in the movie. SEO influences how your website competes in the search engine results so you can outrank your competition where your customers are searching.

Trends in SEO

SEO has changed a lot over the years. It used to be about "tricking" Google by employing a variety of tactics to signal to it that your site is important. Now, search engines are more sophisticated, so tricking them isn't a strategy you should rely on.

Most search strategies today are based on creating a website that has an excellent user experience and incorporating content that people searching would find helpful.

Results Over Time

If you are looking for quick results, SEO is not a great tool to choose. It often takes 6 – 12 months to generate results from search engine optimization efforts.

SEO is about changing (improving) how relevant and important Google thinks your site is for a specific search term or phrase. It can take time to change these perceptions.

SEO is a strategy that should be viewed as a long-term investment. If you invest in the strategies and tactics that work, you'll see results over time.

This isn't a quick fix or an instant results strategy for digital.

Long-term Is about GREAT Content

While there are both strategies and tactics that SEO professionals use to bolster your results, the reality is that in the long-term, sustainable SEO is about great content.

Content sends all the right signals to search engines – it shows that you are authoritative and relevant for the topics that you cover.

The key is that just creating content on your site isn't good enough. The content has to generate traffic, social shares, and most importantly links for Google to view it as important in search results.

More and more businesses are focused on creating relevant content that others share and talk about to build a sustainable SEO strategy. To achieve this, we've seen a shift in focus from volume of content to quality of content. If you create a lot of content that people don't share, it won't drive results. Creating a few pieces of great content that gets significant results is the more sustainable path to success.

Less Keyword Focused

We still talk about keywords in SEO because it's difficult to create a strategy around phrases and questions, but Google is becoming less reliant on them.

As Google has become more sophisticated it does a better job at understanding the intent of a search and connecting the searcher with relevant content.

Strategies like keyword stuffing are not very effective. You do still need to use words and phrases that signal to Google what your website is about, but keywords alone aren't the ticket to success.

Big Idea:
Some people think that there is a link between spending money advertising on Google and organic search engine rankings. There isn't. Google has explicitly stated this, and many search experts have independently validated it.

Mobile is Now

Over 50% of searches happen on mobile devices, which means that every aspect of your SEO strategy must be optimized for mobile.

Specifically, this means making sure that your website is mobile-friendly and also loads quickly. Google will reduce the visibility in search results of websites that load slowly.

Note: We'll cover website speed in the chapter on Websites.

Voice is the Future

Voice search will be the next frontier in digital marketing and specifically in search. Voice devices like Amazon Alexa and Google Home are gaining market share, but also more and more people rely on voice search from their mobile phones.

The challenge with voice search for marketers is that only one result is typically shared in voice search results. This means that the competition to rank first will be even greater.

SEM and SEO

SEM and SEO are sometimes used interchangeably, but they refer to two different aspects of search engine marketing.

SEM stands for Search Engine Marketing and it includes both paid search and organic search. Paid search is ads that you pay to display on Google. SEO is often referred to as organic search, and it focuses on increasing the authority and relevance of your website so that it naturally ranks towards the top of Search Engine Results Pages (SERPs).

As you can see in the image below, search engine results consist of both paid and organic. In general, about 80% of clicks go to organic results and 20% of clicks go to paid.

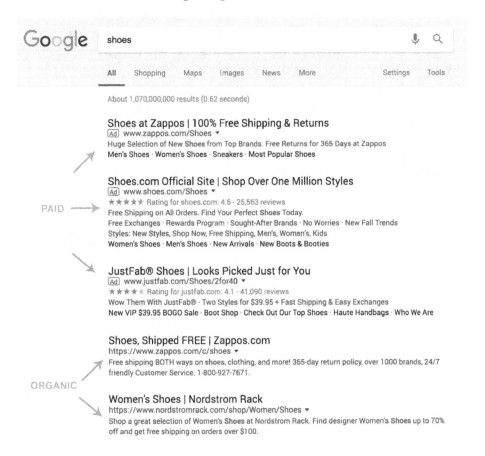

Many businesses use both paid and organic as a part of their strategy. Even if you rank first organically for a term, 20% of the clicks could go to your competitors who advertise. For this reason, search ads are often purchased for important terms, even if the business ranks first organically.

How Search Engines Work

When you search for something, Google searches the web by "crawling" websites to find the most relevant content based on what you searched for. The goal of Google is to bring you the most relevant content based on what you searched for.

The image below gives you a technical overview of how search engines work. If this seems complicated, don't worry. While it's good to have a basic understanding of the mechanics of search engines and key terms, you don't need to understand all of the details to use SEO strategically.

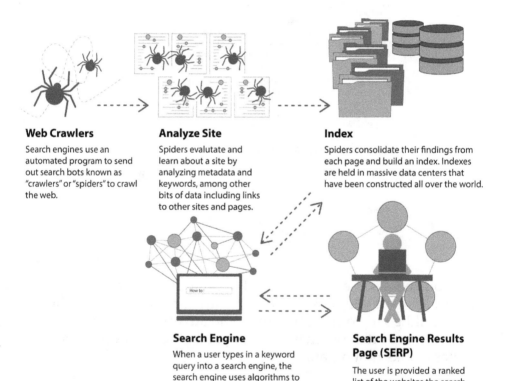

Web Crawlers

Search engines use an automated program to send out search bots known as "crawlers" or "spiders" to crawl the web.

Analyze Site

Spiders evalutate and learn about a site by analyzing metadata and keywords, among other bits of data including links to other sites and pages.

Index

Spiders consolidate their findings from each page and build an index. Indexes are held in massive data centers that have been constructed all over the world.

Search Engine

When a user types in a keyword query into a search engine, the search engine uses algorithms to scour its billions of indexes to pull out the most releveant results.

Search Engine Results Page (SERP)

The user is provided a ranked list of the websites the search engine has determined are the most relevant and most popular.

For most search terms there are MILLIONS of potential websites that Google could show you, so Google must decide which site to show you first.

There are three basic elements that Google uses to determine what you see. We break this down into the ART of SEO – Authority, Relevance, and Technical.

There are actually hundreds, if not thousands, of factors that Google uses in their algorithm to determine which websites they display in SERPs. Google doesn't disclose exactly what these are but gives indicators of what matters to help guide SEO experts.

Authority

For most searches there are millions of websites that could be displayed as the search result. Google looks at the authority of your website when determining how high your site will rank in SERPs.

Authority basically means how important does Google think your website is. Google determines the authority for both your website overall as well as for individual pages. For example, you could have a website that Google feels is pretty important, but individual pages that aren't as important.

So how does Google determine authority? In general Google looks at a variety of factors to determine how important your site is including things like the age of the domain, if your site looks like a legitimate business site, social media profiles, and links.

Links are one of the most important factors in determining the authority of your site. A link is when another website on the internet links to your site, for example a blogger writes about your business and includes a link back to your site.

Tool: ahrefs Link Checker
The ahref Links Check (www.ahrefs.com/backlink-checker) is a free tool that will check the backlinks for any site for you for free. Enter the URL that you want to check, and you can see the number of links and the specific links as well. You can also look at competitors to see how you stack up.

Backlink profile for bootcampdigital.com
Domain with all its subdomains

Domain rating	Backlinks	Referring domains
44	18,938	623
	88% dofollow	71% dofollow

Top 100 backlinks Top 5 anchors Top 5 pages One link per domain

Referring page	DR	UR	Domains	Traffic	Anchor and backlink
The Best Times to Post on Social Media in 2018 Based on Research 🔒 coschedule.com/blog/best-times-to-post-on-social-media/ EN ECOMMERCE WORDPRESS	83	74	1,309	11,880	https://bootcampdigital.com/best-times-to-post-on-social-media-2018/ 🔒 bootcampdigital.com/best-times-to-post-on-social-media-2018/ CONTENT
Krista Neher - Speaker • Best-Selling Author • Entrepeneur • CEO • Digital Marketing Strategy 🔒 kristaneher.com/ EN WORDPRESS	31	32	76	11	https://www.bootcampdigital.com/training 🔒 www.bootcampdigital.com/training ↳ 301 bootcampdigital.com/training
5 Engagement Metrics That'll Help Improve Your Search Rankings 🔒 neilpatel.com/blog/5-engagement-metrics-thatll-help-improve-your-search-rankings/ EN WORDPRESS	90	30	66	1.3	http://bootcampdigital.com/mobile-marketing-stats-2014-infographic/ bootcampdigital.com/mobile-marketing-stats-2014-infographic/ CONTENT

Power Tip:
Compare your links to the links of your competitors. Are they getting links from somewhere that you aren't? Are they using strategies that you can learn from?

When it comes to links, not all links are equal. Links from more important sites count more than links from less important sites. Most links that you place yourself in a directory listing or from an ad don't count at all.

Google and other SEO tools assign a "score" to websites and web pages that show how important they are. These scores are based on a number of factors and aim to replicate how Google determines how important a site is.

In the screenshot from ahrefs you see a number called "Domain Rating" of 44. This means that on a scale of 0 – 100, this website is ranked a 44 in terms of overall authority. You can check the authority for an entire domain or a specific page.

Google has their own rating for this called PageRank. PageRank is on a scale from 0 – 10 with 10 sites being big and powerful sites like Wikipedia, Amazon, or Facebook.

Tool: Page Rank Checker
The site www.checkpagerank.net allows you to check your PageRank to see how important and authoritative Google thinks your site is. A score of 4 and above is good for most businesses.

Power Tip:
Compare your PageRank or Domain Rating to your competitors to see how you stack up. Your aim should be to improve this over time, but it is helpful to know how your authority compares to similar sites.

Relevance

Relevance is about how relevant your site is for a specific term that is searched. Let's say I search for "Healthy Pineapple Cake Recipe." When Google is searching sites to display in search results it will look not only at how important the webpage is, but which webpage seems to be most relevant for the search. While many pages may use different combinations of the words Healthy, Pineapple, Cake and Recipe, Google will aim to find the site that is most relevant to the search.

Relevance comes down to the content on your site. Is your site about what you want to be found for? For example, if you want to be found for Healthy Pineapple Cake Recipe, create a page called Healthy Pineapple Cake Recipe, ideally with the recipe on it, and explain why it's healthy.

Use the phrases and keywords that you want to be found for on your site. Google isn't psychic. If you are a Digital Marketing Training Company like Boot Camp Digital, Google doesn't know that this is what you do if you don't use those words on your site.

 Big Idea: Have a Blog
This is why many websites have a blog – because the blog allows them to create lots of relevant content that signals to Google what their site is about. In addition, many people link to or reference blog posts, so they are powerful in improving your search rankings.

The more important the content surrounding a topic is on your site, the more relevant Google thinks that content is. For example, a page called Digital Marketing Training will signal what the page is about better than calling the page "Services."

When it comes to content, it should be natural – don't try to use words in a way that isn't relevant or natural sounding when you say them out loud. Focus on creating content that is about what you want to be found for.

Power Tip:
To be sure that your site has relevant content, a simple check is to determine the words and phrases that you want your site and/or individual pages to rank for. Check if these words and phrases are used on your site.

Technical

Technical setup basically means that the site is setup in a way that makes it easy for Google to understand the content on it.

In a technical review of your site you'll want to check that your content is organized in a logical way and that you have appropriate sub-pages or category pages as needed to drive search traffic to your site.

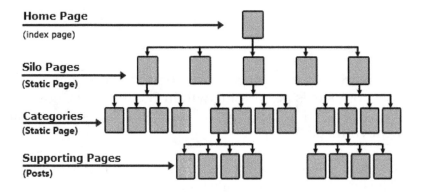

There are many technical aspects to setting up your site correctly including things like making sure you have a sitemap, that your files are readable to search engines, and more. We won't go in to these in detail, but there are tools that you can use to check the technical setup of your site.

Tool: WooRank
WooRank.com is a free site that allows you to check the SEO score for your site. It includes links and content as well as technical audits. WooRank will show you if there are any issues with how your site is setup that will impact your search rankings. Very few sites score perfectly, and you can choose to not have all of the recommended elements present. You can also look up your competitors on WooRank.

It's important to also make sure that Google can read your site and know how your site is performing within Google. The Google Search Console is a free tool that will show you if Google sees any issues with your site.

Search Console will also show you how your site is performing in search. The keyword phrases that send traffic to your site, as well as ranking and volumes, are available to help you understand your overall performance.

Search Console is free but must be setup for your website. Your web developer can make sure that it is added to your site.

Tool: Search Console
Be sure that Google Search Console is setup for your website. This will give you alerts if Google notices something wrong and you can also check search engine traffic and performance.

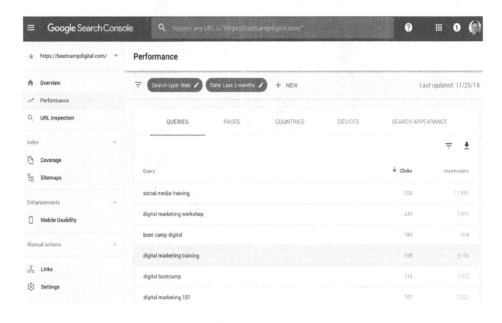

Process of Search Engine Optimization

Now that we know how search engines like Google work, the next step is to optimize your site for them and build your plan for SEO. Whether you choose to DIY or hire an SEO company to help, it's useful to understand the process. SEO can be quite technical, and it this is an important area for your business you may want to hire an expert.

There are five steps in the Process of SEO: Research, Strategy, On-Page, Off-Page, and Measure and Improve.

Step 1: Research

The first step in the process of executing SEO is research. Research and understand the keywords and phrases that drive your business.

For any business there are many keywords that could send highly qualified traffic to your site. The key is to focus on keywords that both send qualified traffic and aren't too competitive based on the authority of your website.

For example, attempting to rank for generic words like "milk" or "social media" will be difficult because high authority sites like Wikipedia already rank for these words and they aren't likely to send great traffic to your site. Instead focus on words that are closer to what someone actively looking for you would search for. For example, "Dairy Alternatives" or "Best Soy Milk."

Power Tip:
You can see all of the websites that have a certain keyword in their title by going to Google and searching for allintitle:keyword (but replace keyword with the keyword or phrase you want to search for). Google will show you all of the pages that use this keyword in the title.

In the keyword research stage your goal is to develop a handful of keywords for your site and for key pages on your site to focus your SEO efforts.

Examine and brainstorm:
- Words that describe your product or service
- Words that have purchase intent
- Words competitors optimize for
- Words that describe the problem your product solves

The Google Keyword Planner tool is the most used tool for keyword analysis. Google will show you search volumes and keyword ideas for you based on your website, competitive websites, or by starting with search terms.

Tool: Google Keyword Planner
The Google Keyword Planner is available within Google Ads (ads.google.com) and you need a Google Ad account to access it. This shows you search volume and competitiveness for search terms. This can be helpful to understand what people are looking for and the words and phrases they use.

Keyword (by relevance)	Avg. monthly searches	Competition	Top of page bid (low range)	Top of page bid (high range)
digital marketing training	720	High	$7.00	$13.08
digital marketing course	2,900	High	$8.40	$27.00
online marketing courses	1,900	High	$13.80	$37.70
marketing courses	1,000	High	$10.05	$15.41
online digital marketing courses	1,000	High	$11.03	$32.30
digital marketing certification	2,400	High	$6.00	$15.00
internet marketing course	390	High	$9.94	$29.40
learn digital marketing	590	High	$6.00	$15.48
online marketing training	170	Medium	$8.80	$21.74
best digital marketing course	210	High	$9.94	$25.00

Power Tip:
You can see the keywords that your competitors have placed in the headers of their website pages by looking at the code. To see the code, choose to view a page in developer mode on your browser.

The goal of keyword research is to have a list of keywords that you will target your site to rank for.

Step 2: Strategy

Once you have an idea of the keywords that could work for your business, it can be helpful to align the keywords to your business or marketing strategy.

What is it that you most want to achieve for your business, and what keywords are appropriate for different stages of the marketing funnel?

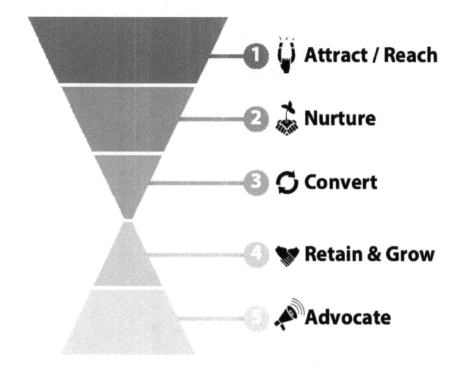

1. Attract / Reach
2. Nurture
3. Convert
4. Retain & Grow
5. Advocate

Since a strong search strategy is able to reach people who are looking to buy or convert, Google recommends a strategy that starts by focusing on the most relevant terms to your brand first, and then breaking out.

Start with **brand** keywords - keywords with your brand or business name or potentially your competitors.
> For example: Tide Laundry, Tide Pods, Tide Liquid, Tide Detergent, as well as competitive terms like Purex, Purex Detergent, etc. (if appropriate)

Next consider **category** keywords –keywords that are directly related to your product and how it is used. The focus here is on your product and its function.
> For example: Best laundry detergent, how to do laundry, organic laundry detergent, etc.

Finally, you may incorporate **affinity** keywords – keywords that are more broadly related to the category that you participate in. These are interests or problems that your keywords can address.
For example: How to remove grass stains, how to soften clothes, how to prevent stains, how to pre-treat clothes, etc.

Remember:

While search works best when it is more directly related to your product, consider your marketing strategy and objectives, and choose an SEO keyword strategy that reflects what you are trying to achieve for your business.

Step 3: On-Page SEO

Once you know your strategy and keywords, the next step is to optimize your site and your site content to signal relevance to Google.

On-page SEO also involves technical setup, but we covered this earlier in the chapter, so here we will focus on the content of the page.

Depending on how your site is structured and the content you already have in place, this may involve optimizing existing content and copy, or you may need to build a strategy to create new content over time.

A few questions to ask yourself:

- Do you have content specifically related to the words you want to rank for?

- Do you have posts on these specific topics?

- Do you have socially sharable content on the topics or keywords you want to rank for?

Step 4: Off-Page SEO

Once your site is relevant, off-site SEO focuses on activities that you can do outside of your website to signal authority to Google.

The focus here is usually on link-building, or getting other sites to link to yours. Some links happen naturally for most businesses, for example when they are featured in the news or members of business associations.

It is good to be deliberate and aware of opportunities to have other websites who mention you link back to your site. If you are serious about SEO, you'll want to have a dedicated link-building strategy.

Step 5: Measure and Improve

Analytics are critical to a successful SEO plan. Google provides lots of tools between Google Analytics and Google Search Console to help you understand if your SEO efforts are generating results.

You can use a variety of sources to understand the performance of your website including:

- **Google Analytics:** To track information about how people get to your site and what they do once they are there. Analytics will help you to understand the quality of the traffic that you are getting from search engines.
- **Google Tag Manager:** To manage tags and track traffic without editing the website code directly.
- **Google Search Console:** To get information about the keywords that are sending traffic to your site and how you rank for them.

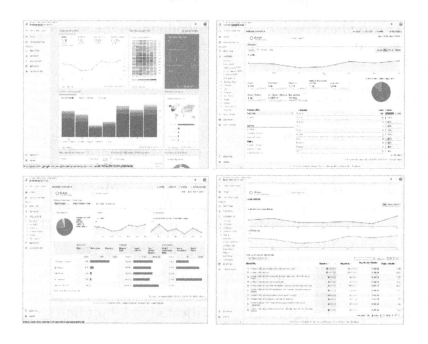

There is a lot of information available about the performance of your website and how you rank for core search terms.

If you are investing in an SEO strategy, set KPIs (Key Performance Indicators) for your search efforts to track the metrics that matter to you.

You may choose to set rankings for specific high-value keywords as a target for your efforts, overall traffic from search, or performance relative to other benchmarks.

Search Engine Optimization

- ➢ How can SEO achieve your business goals?
- ➢ What keywords/phrases do you want to rank for?
- ➢ How can you begin to improve your SEO with Authority, Relevance, Technical optimization?

_____

_____

_____

_____

_____

_____

_____

What is the big thing you want to remember from this chapter?

_____

_____

Go to www.ThatActuallyWorks.com/DigitalMarketing for your free action planner and bonus resources.

Chapter 9: Websites

These days, websites maybe doesn't seem like the most interesting or relevant topic in digital marketing. Today most businesses have a website and it's easier than ever to create one that looks good and has a lot of functionality. But are those sites as effective as they could or should be?

Since the beginning of online marketing, websites have been the core of a business's online presence. Every business (yes, *every business*) needs a strong website.

Trends in Websites

While websites aren't new many marketers think them as an afterthought. A website is still the core of your online presence. Depending on the type of business you are in, it may be vital to your success (for example ecommerce) or a brochure to inspire people to work with you and establish your credibility (for example consultants or CPG brands). In either case your website should be clean and simple to use and employ the best practices that create a great user experience.

Mobile

Most websites experience over 50% of their traffic from mobile. You can't afford to have a site that doesn't work well on mobile devices. We used to talk about mobile optimization, but now you should design for mobile first.

Tool: Google Mobile Friendly Test
Google has a mobile friendly test that will alert you if there are any mobile issues with your site. Common issues are buttons too close together or text unreadable on mobile. Go to search.google.com/test/mobile-friendly to see if Google spots any issues with your site on mobile devices. If you do have issues, address them immediately as they will impact your rankings in mobile search.

Site Speed

Site speed is a big issue that many businesses still ignore. Site speed is important for a number of reasons:
- Slow sites create a bad user experience
- Many people won't wait for a slow website
- With more mobile traffic and slower mobile internet speeds, a slow site load is a huge issue
- Facebook reduces visibility of links that go to slow websites
- Google reduces visibility in search results of slow websites

Research from Google shows how site speed impacts bounce rate, or the probability that someone will leave your site after viewing only one page.

As page load time goes from:

1s to 3s the probability of bounce increases 32%

1s to 5s the probability of bounce increases 90%

1s to 6s the probability of bounce increases 106%

1s to 10s the probability of bounce increases 123%

Google suggests that your site should load in three seconds or less, and a recent study showed that most brand websites take over nine seconds to load!

Your site needs to be fast to compete in the marketplace today. If your site is slow there are a number of optimizations that can be made in terms of how the site is displayed, as well as hosting, however sometimes a site needs to be relaunched in order to address speed issues.

 Tool: Google Site Speed
Google has a free site speed test that will identify any issues that are impacting your website speed. You can run the site speed test for free at https://developers.google.com/speed/pagespeed/insights/ and get details on your site performance.
Note: We'll discuss site speed in more detail later in this chapter.

Clean and Simple Design

Websites go through design trends, as a result most businesses refresh their site every few years as it starts to look dated.

The biggest trend from a design standpoint is clean and simple design.

People spend under eight seconds on a homepage on average. You need to grab their attention and quickly and easily get them moving through the content on your site if you want to have an impact.

Nothing is a Substitute

With Facebook Pages and some directory listing become more robust, some businesses question if they need a website. Can their social media presence substitute for a website?

No.

You always need a website for your business. Business websites are one of the most trusted sources of consumer information. Any presence that isn't your website could be changed by the platform owner. For example, Facebook regularly changes how Pages are displayed, their visibility, and even the functionality available.

Nothing is a substitute for a website and any credible business should have one.

Less is More

If everything is important, nothing is important. As marketers, we have a tendency to want to add too many things to our websites. They quickly become cluttered and lack focus.

Decide on **the most important thing** for your website and each page, and **focus!** Resist the urge to clutter your site with too much content.

Prioritize what matters and be prepared to make tough choices – especially in a large organization.

Your Website Strategy

When it comes to your website (like everything else) – start with strategy! What is it that you want the website to do? Why do people visit your site and what are their expectations? How should your website contribute to your strategic goals?

Many businesses focus most of their website efforts on the design – does it look nice. They end up with a website that looks great but isn't actually effective at driving their business.

Whether you are building a new site or improving an existing one, the following steps will help you clarify your site purpose and effectiveness.

Objective

Start with your objective. Your objective should be what you want your website to do for your business. While it's obvious that you need a website, being focused about how your website can grow your business will increase your effectiveness.

Most sites have an initial objective of providing information, but go deeper. For example, a business with a goal of driving word-of-mouth would create talkable content and sharing calls-to-action on the site. A dentist wanting new patients will have calls-to-action to book an appointment prominently on the site.

Audience

Some businesses make the mistake of assuming that customers are their target audience. In reality, most websites get far more traffic than they have customers.

Who is the audience for your site and what is important to them?

Current Situation

Take some time to evaluate your current website. Look at your Google Analytics to see how people are using it. Evaluate what is working and what isn't.

Also look for behavior that may influence your site content and design. For example, the most popular pages, the pages that people start visiting your site from, or the high-bounce pages (pages where people leave).

Buying Cycle

Determine the content needed for every stage of the buying cycle. Businesses often make the mistake of only focusing on selling or a consultation. Consider who is visiting your site and their readiness for your main call-to-action. Identify why people visit your site and have the right content for them.

Example:
In working with a solar energy company, their only website call-to-action was to get an estimate. It was appropriate for people pretty interested in solar already. When discussing their cycle and audience, they found that under 5% of their website visitors were at that stage and for an estimate. They added Solar 101 content and Money Saving Calculators to

reach people who were further up the funnel. This made their site more relevant to more visitors.

Competition

One of the best things about digital marketing is that you can see exactly what your competitors are doing. Check out the website of your top competitors, especially if they have invested a lot on their site.

Value Proposition

Determine what your value proposition is for your audience beyond the functional features of your product. Consider the **benefits** that drive someone to do business with you, and make sure those also come across.

Some businesses, especially consumer goods businesses that don't sell through their sites, clutter them with promotions and ads but lose site of the value proposition for the consumer.

As you are close to finalizing your website, check that it is helpful to your customer and adding value vs. just promoting your business.

---

3 Areas to an Effective Website

There are three areas to focus on when evaluating or building an effective website – content, design and technical.

Content

The first question is what actually goes on your site?

- **Site Content** – What is the purpose for the site overall? Why do people visit? What needs to be there?
- **Site Structure** – How will the content and pages be organized on the site? How does somebody navigate in an intuitive way to find what he or she needs?
- **Page Content** – Each individual page, including the home page, should have a clear strategy and purpose.

For both your site and each page ask yourself:
- What do you want somebody to do?
- What do they want from each page?
- What do you want to drive them to do?

When you have a clear answer to each of those questions, you'll move on to evaluating your content. Ask yourself:
- Is it instantly obvious what your business does?
- It is clear what category you operate in?
- Is the content relevant to the audience?
- Is it concise but useful?

Big Idea: Every Page Matters
Keep in mind that not all website traffic will enter your site through your home page, so every page should be clear as an initial entry page. You can check your most popular entry pages in Google Analytics.

Design

The design focuses on how your content is brought to life and how the website actually looks. Website design does follow trends, and most businesses refresh their design every three years or so to keep it looking modern.

A strong website design should meet the following criteria:
- Clear call-to-action

- Key information is easy to find
- Consistent with brand
- Relevant to audience
- Engaging and relevant visuals.

 Big Idea: Intuitive Experience
The design should facilitate a seamless consumer experience. The goal of your design should be that people can find what they need without having to think. It should be obvious where to find things.

As you evaluate the design of your site, you can use the seven elements of UX (User Experience). User experience is the practice of creating a great (simple) experience for your visitors.

Useful – The site should have content that is of use to the audience – it should fulfill a need and provide value to the visitor.

Usable – The site should be easy to use and complete tasks. No guesswork.

Findable – Search and the site navigation should make content easy to find.

Credible – Make sure your site comes across as credible by aligning with branding, having professional visuals, and incorporate testimonials, client lists, and more.

Desirable – Know your key value proposition and make it stand out! Use copy and images that make people HAVE TO HAVE it!

Accessible – This is a technical area, but the site should work on all browsers and also be accessible to people with disabilities.

Valuable – The site should add value to your audience. Give them helpful content, tutorials, or tips.

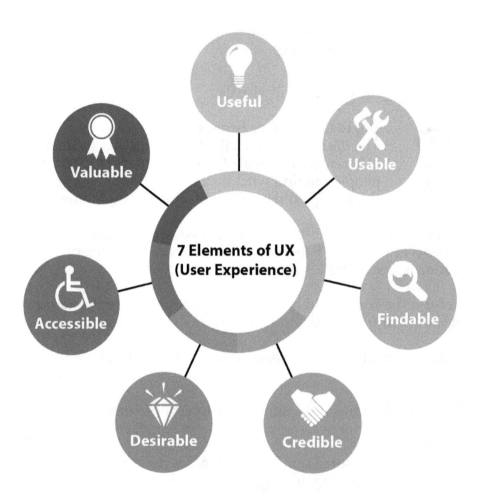

When it comes to user experience, follow established practices of what people expect from a website.

Technical

Technical refers to how the site is set up technically. We won't get in to too much detail here, since the focus of this book is on marketing, but it is helpful to have some understanding of the technical choices to make.
Site Platform and Setup

There are three main ways that businesses build websites – Website Builder, Wordpress or Open Source Platform, and Custom Development.

1) **Website Builder** – There are many free platforms where businesses can easily create their own website – as simple as dragging and dropping content. GoDaddy and Google both offer website builders. These are great for small businesses just starting out, but they aren't very flexible. They are cheap and easy, but will be limited in functionality.

2) **Wordpress or Open Source Platform** – There are open source platforms like Wordpress that are free for businesses to use to create their websites on. Most businesses use a website platform like Wordpress (which is the leading website platform in the world) to make it easier to manage the technical aspects of their website.

   What makes Wordpress or another platform powerful is that you can easily make changes to your site without having to call a developer and it is also easy to add functionality through plugins. These platforms are both cost-effective and flexible.

3) **Custom Development** – Fewer businesses opt to build their own site unless they are a platform-based business, meaning their site is the service. Custom sites are expensive and difficult to maintain.

Site Speed
As explained earlier, site speed is really important. A slow site is usually caused by:
- **Server setup** – Having a slow server or one that isn't powerful enough can result in a slow site speed. This would be caused by the host of your site.

- **Technical setup** – There are aspects of the technical setup of your website that can slow it down. This is usually driven by how content is coded and set up on the site.
- **Content** – Content is a leading cause of slow sites. This includes things like images that are large and take time to load, as well as too much content or too many plugins or tags on the site slowing it down.

If you aren't a technical expert it can be challenging to understand what is driving a slow site. There are free tools that give an overview of site speed and how to fix it. The Google site speed tool (discussed earlier) gives some information but there are also more detailed tools.

Tool: GT Metrix Site Speed
It is free to generate a report on www.GTMetrix.com and it gives you a breakdown of site speed and the details of what is slowing it down. This can be a strong starting point to discuss with your web developer.

Secure
A secure site has https:// at the front of the URL instead of just http – the "s" stands for secure.

Some browsers like Google Chrome will block your site if it isn't secure. This is easy to setup and is usually done by the company who does your web hosting.

SEO
Your site should be technically optimized for search engines to help them understand your content and grow your visibility in search engine results.

Analyzing Your Website

The only way to know how your site is performing is to look at analytics. Google Analytics is the most popular analytics tool and it's free. Most web developers install it automatically, or it can be added by just placing some code on the site.

Power Tip:
Set up analytics on your site immediately – even if you don't have time to use it right away. Analytics will not be able to show historical data from before it was installed.

Website analytics doesn't just tell you how your website is performing. If you have other digital marketing efforts that send people to your site – like ads, social media, or emails – you can track their effectiveness through analytics.

Analytics gives you insights about your website in a few different areas.

Audience – This gives you information about your audience – the people coming to your site. Google provides a lot of information about your audience including demographics and their interests.

Behavior – The behavior section gives you information about how people behave on your site. You can view top pages/content as well as time on site and userflows for your site.

Acquisition – This shows you how people get to your site. Many businesses focus on traffic, but ignore the quality of traffic. Acquisition data shows where your traffic comes from and gives you information about how high quality that traffic is.

Conversions – It is helpful to set up "conversions" on your site to understand how it's *really* performing. A conversion is an action that you track. It can be sales, visiting a contact page, signing up for an email, or any goal that your website has. If conversions are set up, you can track what drives conversions and the behavior of converters.

Power Tip:
Build a plan to check analytics regularly – it is easy to forget. Set a weekly, monthly, or quarterly appointment (depending on your capacity and the size and importance of your site) to check in on your analytics.

Optimizing Your Website

Optimizing websites is about adapting or changing your site to improve its performance.

Landing Pages

Landing pages are often used to improve site performance – especially when there is a specific action that you want to drive.

A landing page is a page on the website that has a clear focus on a specific objective, and often other website information is removed to minimize distractions. For example, most landing pages don't even have the website navigation, header, or footer so that the main action (filling out the form or buying a product) is the focus.

Landing pages are often used as a part of an online advertising strategy. Rather than sending traffic to your homepage or other area of your site with distractions, if the goal is to generate leads, traffic may be sent to a lead page focused on getting a form completed.

The advantage of using a landing page is that it often leads to higher conversion rates. Landing pages can also be tested and improved to grow results over time.

Conversion Optimization

Conversion optimization is the task of improving a conversion rate over time. The conversion rate is the percent of people who visit a website and take a desired action – or convert. A conversion could be a sale, an email for completion, placing a phone call, or taking any other action.

Conversion rate optimization is about changing and improving your website, usually through testing, to improve your conversion rate.

Big Idea: Make it Stand Out
The best strategy to drive conversions is to make sure that your call-to-action stands out and is prominent on the page. It should be towards the top, clearly visible, and have a strong value proposition to drive the action.

Many people want to know the best practices or tricks to improve conversion rates. Some studies show, for example, that a green button works best. While that may be true most of the time, it isn't always.

The one thing that most conversion experts agree on is that the only way to know what works best for you is to test.

A/B Testing

While there are many best practices, the best way to know is to test. Testing your website allows you to make small changes to see if the change impacts your results.

In order to test, you must have a clear idea of the goal of your page and what you want to test. For example, on a page focused on driving a purchase, the goal is BUY. I may test button colors or the order of content on a page. Alternately my goal could be email signups and I could test two different free bonuses to drive that.

A/B testing can be used to test any element of your site. Headlines, colors, calls-to-action, text, content, navigation, fonts, and images can all be tested.

Testing is simple as there are a number of tools designed to make it easy. Using these tools, you can create multiple versions of your site, with each version randomly shown to different people to see what best drives action.

Tool: Google Optimize A/B Testing
Google has an A/B testing tool (optimize.google.com) that creates different versions of your site and checks response rates. This is built into Google and easy to use.

Tool: Optimizely
Optimizely.com is a popular website optimization tool because it is quick and easy to use and does the analysis for you. This tool is a great way to constantly optimize your site by creating different tests over time.

Ecommerce

Ecommerce has opened the door for businesses to sell their products online directly to their customers. Billion-dollar businesses are built online through ecommerce sites.

When it comes to ecommerce there are four options on how to execute it: Selling through third party sites, selling through an ecommerce platform, adding ecommerce software on your site, or creating your own ecommerce site.

Businesses may use more than one of the options below at once.

Third Party Ecommerce Sites

Third-party ecommerce sites are sites like Amazon, eBay, and Etsy where businesses can create an account and start selling their products on the site.

The advantage of these platforms is that they are very easy to get started. The disadvantage is that you have to stand out in a crowded marketplace and drive demand for your product.

The focus of efforts on a third-party ecommerce site is to make your products look as appealing as possible and generate demand. Most businesses focus on optimizing their listings and using digital marketing to drive traffic to them.

Ecommerce Platforms

There are ecommerce websites where you can use their platform to create your own "shop" on another website. Shopify is among the most popular of these types of sites.

On sites like Shopify businesses can setup a store by uploading products and using templates to customize the website. The advantage of this is you can have your own ecommerce platform quickly. The downside is that it isn't as flexible as having your own site.

When creating your own site on these platforms you'll need to focus on all aspects of website setup and design to make your site come to life. The upside is that these sites have templates to make it easy. Businesses can be up and running in as little as a few hours.

Ecommerce Software on Your Site

If you have a website that already exists or want the control of your own site there is software that can be used to add ecommerce to your site. The most popular platforms for this are Magento Cart, and WooCommerce.

This software takes care of the heavy lifting in terms of coding and setup, but does still require some development efforts.

The advantage of this option is that it is easier to execute and has a lot of flexibility. The challenge is that it can be more complex to implement vs. Shopify. Many medium to large enterprises choose this option for ecommerce, as it is a good balance of flexibility and simplicity.

Customized Ecommerce Site

The most challenging option to execute is to create your own ecommerce site. This is rarely done since there are many solid and flexible ecommerce platforms existing.

That being said, if ecommerce is your core competency you can build your own platform. This would be very expensive and time consuming.

Websites

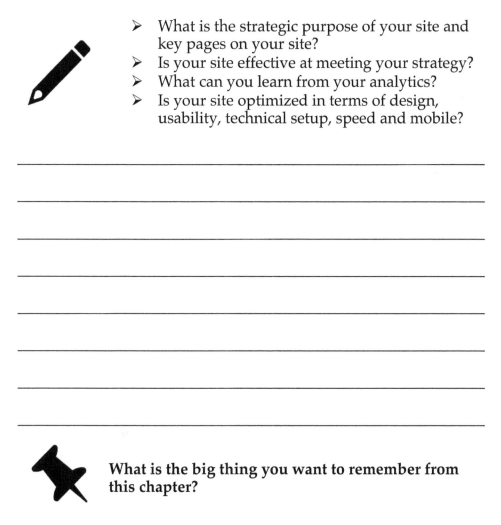

- ➢ What is the strategic purpose of your site and key pages on your site?
- ➢ Is your site effective at meeting your strategy?
- ➢ What can you learn from your analytics?
- ➢ Is your site optimized in terms of design, usability, technical setup, speed and mobile?

_____

_____

_____

_____

_____

_____

_____

What is the big thing you want to remember from this chapter?

_____

_____

Go to www.ThatActuallyWorks.com/DigitalMarketing for your free action planner and bonus resources.

Chapter 10: Conversational Marketing

Conversational marketing is marketing focused at driving conversations or harnessing influencers or partners to promote your business, usually in conversations.

Conversational marketing includes a number of different core digital marketing strategies:
- Influencer marketing
- Ratings and reviews
- Community management
- Online public relations
- Online word-of-mouth
- Employee Advocacy

When it comes to digital marketing many businesses are so focused on posting their own content that they forget to harness the power of others to spread their message.

On almost any study word-of-mouth shows up as a top influencer of purchases, yet it is rarely seen on digital marketing plans.

Word-of-mouth is also one of the most trusted forms of marketing. People are more trusting of recommendations from strangers than they are of most marketing methods.

Krista Neher

As the chart below from the Nielsen consumer trust survey shows, the top three trusted sources are recommendations and referrals.

TOP 3 TRUSTED SOURCES

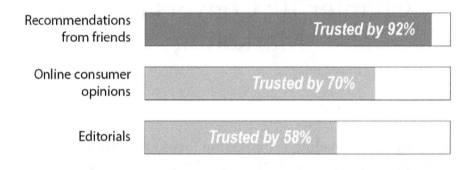

Recommendations from friends — Trusted by 92%

Online consumer opinions — Trusted by 70%

Editorials — Trusted by 58%

Influencer Marketing

What is Influencer Marketing?

Influencer marketing is when businesses partner with people online who have a large following as a way to gain exposure to their audience. Typically a business compensates an "influencer." In return the influencer promotes the brand based on agreed upon terms.

Influencer marketing can work for B2B and B2C businesses. While many B2B businesses don't think about influencers, we recently ran a two day Influencer Workshop for a medical device company that wanted to help their influencers create and share better content online. The brand has been able to trace measurable sales back to the influencers that they partner with.

Influencer marketing is almost like a celebrity endorsement, but instead of you promoting the celebrity to your own audience, the celebrity is promoting to their audience.

Online influencer marketing isn't new. It has been around for over 10 years, since the early days of social media. It continues to be an in-demand and high-growth area of digital marketing.

Why Businesses Use Influencers

Influencers are popular with marketers because it allows them to reach new audiences in a way that is trusted by the audience.

Organic Social Media Reach
Many businesses struggle to gain organic reach on Facebook, so working with Influencers is a way for them to reach people in the feed.

Some influencers can reach millions of people, but even smaller influencers often reach tens of thousands. Their posts are in the news feeds of the people that you want to reach.

Influencers Make Great Content
Often influencers are able to make better content vs. brands. An influencer's business relies on creating content that their audience loves. That's win-win for both the business and influencer.

Many influencers are able to come up with creative and compelling ways to share their experience with a brand or a product. The result is often better content vs. what businesses are creating themselves.

Endorsement from the Influencer
Influencers are also a powerful tool because their followers trust them. Since they will often try to integrate your product naturally into their posts, you are essentially gaining an endorsement.

Example:
Seth Godin, a famous marketer shared an anecdote in his blog a number of years ago. He said that when he promotes his own books, he generates only a few sales, but when he promotes other people's books he generates tons of sales. This is because a recommendation or endorsement is much more powerful vs. promoting something yourself.

Reaching the Influencers Network
One of the biggest advantages of influencer marketing is that you gain exposure to a new audience – the audience of the influencer. One of the big challenges online is getting your message in front of the right audience. If you choose your influencers well, they are probably already in front of the people that you want to reach. By partnering with them your business is exposed to a new audience.

Influencers Can Drive Sales
Some fashion and beauty brands have started to rely heavily on influencers to sell their products. Even though you can't share clickable links in Instagram, the power of seeing people rave about a product is huge.

Example:
In 2015 the UK department store Lord & Taylor made headlines as they paid 50 Instagram influencers to wear a specific dress – which sold out in a single weekend!

How to Work with Influencers

There are a few different models that businesses use when working with influencers. For brands wanting to run large-scale influencer programs there are agencies that specialize in working with them.

1. **Simple Quid pro Quo**
   The easiest form of influencer marketing is a quick and simple exchange. Typically the influencer creates a post (or a number of posts) for a set fee or free product. Most influencers charge a fee or require a high-value free product.

   The advantage of this approach is that it is relatively easy to execute and the results are clear. The disadvantage is that the influencer is not really committed to your brand or business, and may just as easily sell their next post to your competitor. Additionally, if influencers don't actually use and love your products their posts may come across as less authentic and not achieve the desired results.

2. **Influencer Events**

   Rather than doing a set exchange, some businesses will create exclusive events or experiences for influencers. Many local businesses now do this when they have a new opening or new product launch.

   For example, a new grocery store invited bloggers to a VIP food tasting with a local chef to build excitement for their grand opening.

   B2B and CPG marketers sometimes do events like this as well. In the earliest days of influencer marketing many large brands like Johnson & Johnson, Lays, and P&G created VIP events where they invited influencers to their offices or factories for a part business, part fun experience. Many B2B companies host Influencer VIP events as a part of major industry conferences, or invite influencers to exclusive conferences of their own.

The goal of events like this is to begin to build relationships with influencers and get them passionate and excited about your products. These events can be very effective, but they may also be expensive to execute and difficult to maintain momentum after the initial event.

3. **Activate Already Fans**

   One approach to influencer marketing that aims to build long-term loyalty is to find ways to activate or incentivize people who are already fans of your product or service.

   Many years ago I was at a VIP party at a major tech event, and I wrote a blog post about the event and commented about how amazing the chairs where. They had these awesome beanbag chairs called Love Sacs. Love Sac reached out to me and offered to send me a chair free. No strings attached. I'm sure they researched my audience and me first. I was so excited because it was a product I already LOVED, so I posted about it non-stop for days. They earned many high-quality impressions for the price of a chair.

By finding people who already love your product and encouraging or incentivizing them to talk about your business you can create lasting, raving fans.

4. **Long-term Relationship**
   The most effective but most difficult form of influencer marketing is to create long-term relationships with a handful of relevant influencers.

   This typically involves finding people who have similar values and are passionate about your product area, and ideally your product, then working with them collaboratively over a set period of time.

   Asics, the running shoe brand has a program like this where they "sponsor" a handful of fitness enthusiast each year. The selected participants get free products, free registration in races, and other VIP perks in return for sharing their love of Asics.

   Wal-Mart pioneered this type of program with their 11 Moms group. They worked hand-in-hand with a small group of influencers who they promoted, sponsored to attend events, and connected with other opportunities. In return the influencers promoted Wal-Mart and shared specials and products they loved from the stores.

   A few years ago I was approached by a social media tool company. They had read an article where I recommended them and offered to formalize a relationship. They paid me a set amount of money per month and in return I wrote a blog post for them and promoted them as appropriate through my speaking and training programs. It was a natural fit. They gained lots of exposure and I promoted a product I already loved.

These types of formal long-term relationships can be difficult to execute, but they often have the best payout in the long run. Brands are establishing loyal influencers who love them instead of simply a transactional relationship.

Remember:
In any type of partnership-style marketing, having relationships with people is vital to your success. Even in a quid pro quo exchange, having established relationships with people in the industry will maximize your chances of success. Many influencers are regularly pitched by business, so getting them to want to work with you can be a challenge unless you pay really well. Take the time to establish relationships when you can.

Pro Tips for Influencer Marketing

1. **Legal disclosures** – In the US and many other countries influencers are required to disclose that they are compensated for their posts. Businesses can actually be held liable if they compensate influencers - even with free products – without that full disclosure in the promotion. This can be accomplished with a simple hashtag #Ad or #Sponsored.

2. **Provide some guidelines** – It's helpful for brands to provide some guidelines while not stifling creativity. If you are paying for posts you want the influencer to integrate your product into their content in a natural and authentic way. Give them some guidelines and inspiration.

3. **Encourage influencers to be creative** – Don't limit creativity by being too prescriptive. I've seen some influencer campaigns where companies have written posts for the influencers, and the posts usually don't perform well. Influencers are GREAT content creators. Encourage them to

be creative and ask them to share ideas and brainstorming for posts that will achieve your goals and resonate with their audience. Canned content isn't usually a great solution for influencers.

4. **Know your influencers and their audiences** – There are MANY "influencers" who buy their audiences or have a lot of fake followers. Make sure you do some diligence on your influencer partners. It is common to ask for analytics or conduct follower analysis.

5. **Cost of working with influencers** – The cost to work with influencers varies depending on the size of the influencer and the number of brands doing influencer marketing in that space. Parent influencers (mom bloggers) are often heavily courted by brands. B2B influencers are usually pitched fewer opportunities. It is important to start with a conversation to align on expectations.

6. **REMEMBER that influencers earn a living** – Many influencers earn a living from their blog, Instagram account, or YouTube channel. Don't expect them to work for free or for free products unless you have a really high value product. Many influencer outreach programs fail because the business fails to offer something valuable enough to the influencer.

Ratings and Reviews

Ratings and reviews have HUGE potential to help – or hurt – your business. Every business in every industry should have a strategy for ratings and reviews. They are highly trusted by customers and are a key influencer in driving conversions.

People rely on reviews to decide which movies to watch, what to buy, B2B software to use, and for almost any other decision. We trust other people much more than we trust advertisers.

Why Do Reviews Matter?

Studies show that:
- 84% of people give online reviews the same consideration as a personal recommendation.
- 90% of consumers form an opinion about a business based on less than ten reviews.
- 74% of people trust a business more based on positive reviews.

When conducting an online search, business or product, reviews typically show up directly in search results, along with the star ratings.

For many businesses, the business name + reviews is a common search term showing that people are actively looking for reviews.

boot camp digital	🎤 🔍
boot camp digital **reviews**	
best digital **marketing bootcamp**	
digital **marketing bootcamp nyc**	
digital **marketing bootcamp online**	

Your Reviews Strategy

Every business should have a strategy to generate positive reviews. In sports they say the best defense is a good offense – this is true with online reviews as well.

Where Reviews Happen

Reviews can take place and be displayed in many different places online. Based on your industry and business you may use one or more of these sources of reviews to establish your credibility.

On Your Website
Reviews and testimonials are a part of most websites. Almost every site you see has a review or testimonial strategy to build trust and close sales. You can also solicit reviews or testimonials on your site – this functionality is especially common for ecommerce sites.

Facebook
Facebook Pages that are set as local businesses (where people go into the business) have reviews. Facebook often shows up at the top of search results and if you have a star rating the star will display directly in the search engine results, as you can see in the image below.

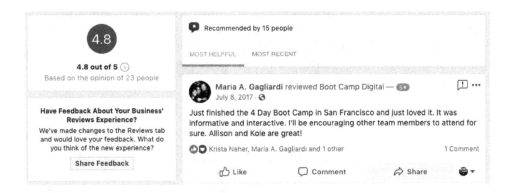

Google
If you have a Google My Business listing, reviews are a key part of your listing and important in building your credibility with Google. Many positive reviews can lead to higher rankings in Google local search results.

Boot Camp Digital ☆ | Website | Directions

5.0 ★★★★★ 5 Google reviews

Marketing consultant in Cincinnati, Ohio

Career Rating Sites

I recently worked with a B2B business and when you searched their name the first thing that appeared after their business sites was a 1 star rating on a site where employees rate their employer. Even if hiring and recruiting aren't a part of your strategy, having strong ratings on career sites can represent your company positively.

Industry Specific Sites

There are rating and review sites for almost every niche or industry. From Rate My Professor to Yelp to Trip Advisor to Software Reviews to Dentist Reviews there are review sites for everything. Know which review sites matter for your business and make sure that you are positively represented there.

Association Sites

Reviews may also appear on trade or association web sites. For example, the BBB (Better Business Bureau) has a reviews section in addition to their complaints and ratings. Check for relevant association sites that have positive listings.

Power Tip:
Do a search for your business name + reviews and your competitor name + reviews to see what shows up. This can give you ideas of the review sites to target for your business.

Getting Positive Reviews

Some businesses assume that if they have a good product or service word will spread and they will generate positive reviews. This isn't the case. Businesses that want to create a powerful and positive online presence must have a proactive strategy to generate positive reviews.

When it comes to reviews remember that the best defense is a good offense. Aim to generate positive reviews so that if (or when) you get a negative review it is offset by positive reviews and doesn't impact your overall star rating. Many businesses go into crisis mode when they have a single negative review that impacts their overall rating. If you have many positive reviews, the negative ones won't be so impactful.

Power Tip:
Avoid the temptation to leave fake positive reviews! In the US the FTC has fined businesses and agencies for leaving reviews without disclosing that there is a conflict. Many review sites (like Google and Facebook) require profiles and have algorithms to detect fake reviews. It is also unethical. Invest the time and effort to generate positive reviews – it pays off!

To generate positive reviews for your business there is a 4-step process that you can use.

1) **Identify the Sites to Target**
There are many review sites that you could target. Start with

one site that ranks well in search engines, and once you've built some reviews there, move on to the next site.

For most businesses Google, Facebook, Yelp, GlassDoor, The Better Business Bureau and LinkedIn (for personal professional recommendations) are good sites to target.

2) **Determine Your Ideal Number of Reviews**
Decide how many reviews you want to target for your business to have a clear goal in mind. At a minimum aim for ten reviews to generate enough reviews to have an impact.

Beyond that look at how many reviews your competitors have, how many reviews it takes on the site to display a rating, and choose a realistic number based on the size of your business and the number of customers you have.

3) **Ask for Reviews!**
You don't get what you don't ask for. As a starting point make a deliberate effort to generate your target number of reviews. This will give you a base of positive reviews to start with.

Some tips for generating positive reviews:

- Ask people personally vs. through a mass email
- Set a clear goal – for example ask three people a week
- Build your reviews over time – most sites show the date a review was left. You want your review profile to look authentic so don't aim for too many reviews in a short time period.
- Tell them EXACTLY where you write a review and how.
- Include a link to make it easy.
- Make your request personal and authentic.

Ask happy customers or long-term/repeat customers and clients first. Let them know you are working on your online presence and that it would mean a lot for you.

Power Tip:
Most websites have terms of service that prohibit businesses from incentivizing reviews. That means that you can't offer a discount or incentive for a positive review.

4) **Operationalize a Review Process**
Build a strategy to ask for reviews on a regular basis. This will help your presence to grow over time. To do this, start with a touchpoint analysis where you look at all of your interactions with clients or customers. Next determine which part of the experience represents the best time to request a review. When are they at the height of their experience with you? Consider segmenting the ask – make sure that you are asking people who will leave a positive review.

Example:
A number of years ago I worked with a dentist who had over 100 reviews on Google and showed up first in search results. It wasn't because he was the best dentist. He used a service to email review requests to happy patients after their appointment. By having a system to generate reviews he grew his positive reviews and his business over time.

Dealing with Negative Reviews

Even for the best businesses, negative reviews happen and are a part of being in business. The most important thing when you have a negative review is to respond as quickly and professionally as possible. Most people don't leave a negative review online as their first step in trying to resolve an issue. Often it happens after they feel that they weren't heard by your business.

Below are some tips for dealing with negative reviews.

1. Keep it professional – While it's tempting to defend yourself or recount the details of the customer's behavior during the experience in question, it's rarely a good look. No one ever wins when debating online. Keep your answer courteous and polite.

2. Don't get defensive – While you may be right, defending your business at all costs is rarely a good strategy. Step back, try to see the situation from the customer point-of-view, and cool off before responding.

3. Respond quickly – Even if you are just looking into it, the longer people wait for an answer the more upset they get. While you may be researching a solution let the reviewer know – otherwise they may feel ignored and continue to escalate.

4. Respond Personally – Canned responses can be infuriating and make the commenter or reviewer feel ignored. Make your response personal so that it is clear that you actually care.

5. Directly Address the Issue – Don't dance around the issue or use generalities. Address it as directly and specifically as possible. This shows that you care.

6. Empathize without admitting fault – Show empathy for the other person's situation. You'd be frustrated too if you waited on hold for two hours, got the wrong order, found an error with a consultant report, or fill-in-the-blank. You can empathize without admitting fault so the person feels heard.

7. Always offer a public response in the same channel – When you can, offer a public response in the same channel. This allows OTHER PEOPLE to see that you care and are responsive. Even if you can't win over the reviewer, your customers will see the review and observe how you handled it. If you got a comment on

Facebook, respond on Facebook – don't try to push the dialogue to your website.

8. Do your best to take it off-line – Offer to call the reviewer, ask the reviewer to call you, or suggest they stop in to talk to a manager. You don't want endless back and forth. Words on a screen are subject to dramatic interpretation. Real people having a real conversation resolve problems. Plus, by publicly offering to connect with the reviewer you convey that you're interested in hearing about their experience and you're making yourself available to them.

9. Have a few templates ready to deploy – Have a few standard responses ready, but make sure that your response doesn't sound canned. Most people want to be heard, so be authentic and directly address their comment.

10. When you don't have anything nice to say, don't say anything at all – Your mom wasn't wrong. When you've attempted to reach out to the reviewer, yet they continue to berate you online, don't engage.

11. Know if Review Sites Can be Updated – Some sites can be updated after the initial review. If you have a bad review but you make it right, consider asking the person to update their review if you are able to turn things around.

Power Tip:
Respond to EVERY review (positive or negative). This reinforces that you care about your customers. Even for the negative reviews, your response is publicly viewable – so even if you can't salvage the negative review you can minimize the impact on your reputation. People don't expect businesses to be perfect, but they expect them to handle negative situations well.

Community Management

Community management is about building, encouraging, and participating in discussions online related to your business, product or industry.

Online community manager

An online community manager builds, grows, and manages online communities, performing Community management, often around a brand or cause. **Wikipedia**

People also search for: Public Relations, Management, MORE

Community management is about relationships. With strong community management a brand seizes the opportunity to interact with people online in public spaces.

The idea of community management is that by engaging in conversations and participating in discussions you will build relationships with people and they will have more affinity towards your product or business.

Why Businesses Do Community Management

Businesses typically engage in community management with an aim of growing brand affinity (people like your business more) or growing advocacy (getting people talking about your business).

Community management is a longer-term strategy to build a brand or businesses that is invested in relationships with people.

If you are looking to drive quick or immediate transactions, or want to build more awareness with many people, community management probably isn't your best choice.

Big Idea: Relationships Count
Sometimes we view digital as a transactional medium and get really focused on driving immediate sales. Relationships matter for your business – they can lead to PR, partnerships, opportunities and more. Consider online relationship building as a part of your business strategy overall.

What are the Goals of Community Management

Community management can take place in a number of places – on your website, on social networks, on YouTube, on discussion forums, and even comments sections of articles or news sites. Community management happens wherever people talk about you or your industry.

Most community managers have set objectives including:
- Managing complaints and compliments
- Turning customers into loyal fans
- Driving brand advocacy
- Developing relationship with influencers
- Building relationships with potential partners
- Networking with other brands or associations
- Generating product feedback
- Providing helpful information
- Responding to positive and negative reviews or comments
- Becoming an industry-recognized expert

What is Involved in Community Management

Community management usually involves four core activities: Monitoring, Engaging, Moderating, and Measuring. The amount of time and energy invested in each will depend on how big your business is, how many customers you have, how many people are already talking about you, and your business goals.

1) **Monitoring** – The first step is to monitor and track conversations online related to your brand, competitors, and industry. Most businesses should invest in this step to understand their customers and how they are perceived.
2) **Engaging** – Engaging involves joining in conversations, initiating conversations, and proactively participating in conversations that relate to your business. The aim of this is to build the reputation of your business and build stronger relationships with customers.
3) **Moderating** – If you have your own social media profiles or other places where you encourage conversations, you'll need to moderate the discussions. This involves determining which comments or discussions add value and which need to be removed or modified. For example many groups have to maintain strict rules about self-promotion to ensure that the group continues to be valuable.
4) **Measuring** – In order to know if your efforts are driving impact, analyzing your performance is important. Consider the goals of your community management efforts upfront and measure what matters based on your goal. Consider both quantitative and qualitative metrics. For example the number of mentions is good to track, but also the sentiment and impact.

The amount of time or resources to invest in community management depends on your business characteristics, your industry, and the results you want.

Big Idea: Set KPIs
It is helpful to set clear KPIs for community management up front so you have clear targets and expectations. This will also allow your community manager to focus their efforts on the metrics that are most important to your business success.

Responding to Comments Online

Monitoring and responding to online comments or mentions should be a part of any social media or online strategy. Any brand with a presence online should have notifications in place to know when they are mentioned and determine how to reply.

Businesses often spend a lot of resources to build a presence online but then drop the ball by not responding to comments or responding late.

Power Tip:
Respond to EVERY comment or mention, or at the very least give it a "like". Your responses are public – show that you appreciate interactions!

If you are active online or have a business that generates mentions, consider implementing the following basic community management principles.

1) **Get Notifications** – Get notifications when people mention your business. You may need to get notifications for multiple channels or networks.
2) **Know Who Will Respond** – Have someone responsible for responding to comments or mentions. It can also be helpful to set an ideal response time so that there are clear expectations.
3) **Establish a Tone of Voice** – If you have someone responding on-the-go on behalf of your business it is

important to be sure that your business is represented consistently and appropriately.

4) **Create Policies or Guidelines** – Create guidelines for responding. A quick review of your customer service and sales questions will give you a feel for what you are most likely to encounter online. Use these as a starting point to build some general guidelines about what to respond to and how to respond.

5) **Know When To Escalate** – Sometimes a community manager can't respond or a difficult situation arises. Know when to escalate or get a second opinion.

6) **Have FUN!** – Don't take yourself too seriously. Have fun and participate in an authentic way.

Old Spice ✅   9 Jul 12
@OldSpice

Why is it that "fire sauce" isn't made with any real fire? Seems like false advertising.

Taco Bell ✅   🐦 Follow
@tacobell

@OldSpice Is your deodorant made with really old spices?

10:52 PM - 9 Jul 2012

↩   ⟲ 1,042   ♥ 782

Tool: Social Media Management
Consider using a tool for community management. There are many that will bring all of your mentions onto a dashboard and allow you to respond from one place. Hootsuite is a popular choice for small businesses, Sprout Social is a good choice for medium businesses and Sprinklr is popular for enterprises.

There are hundreds (maybe thousands) of social media management tools, each with different strengths, weaknesses, and price points. Based on your site and need, evaluate the features to see what works best for you.

Creating Your Own Community

Some businesses want to take their community management efforts to the next level by creating their own community online. Creating your own community online is a big investment and should be considered carefully.

There are two risks with creating your own community. The first is that you create a community and nobody joins. This can result in a waste of time and resources. The second challenge is that the community grows and has lots of members and participation. The challenge with this is that it can take a lot of resources to manage and moderate to be sure that the group stays impactful. Some online groups rely on 10+ moderators for 10K – 20K participants.

When creating your own community or group, it's also helpful to consider if you want to create the community on your own site or use an existing site. For example, some businesses create their own community portal on their site, while others create groups on Facebook or LinkedIn to build their community.

Creating a community on your own site can be difficult and expensive. The challenge is that you need a good enough value proposition for people to specifically visit your site, login, and participate.

Using a social network as the basis of your community has the advantage of being easier to set up. In addition, since people are already on the social network, participating in the community is often easier. The downside is that your community is at the mercy of the social network. For example, if Facebook makes changes to how groups work, your group will be impacted.

Consider if creating a group or community is right for your business. Before jumping in be sure that you have a clear value proposition for your audience and consider polling some customers to gauge interest.

Big Idea: Join Communities!
Prior to even considering creating your own community, start by participating in other communities. You may find that it is easier and more effective to participate in existing communities vs. creating your own.

Online Public Relations

Public relations (PR) happens everywhere – both online and offline. That being said there are two areas to consider with respect to public relations and digital marketing. The first is to make sure that your PR assets and presentation is suitable for online mentions and articles. The second is to take advantage of the unique opportunities that the digital space provides for PR – including working with bloggers or smaller publications and harnessing open-publishing news sites.

There are a few trends in PR that have been fueled by digital that you can take advantage of.

- **24-hour news cycle** – News now happens 24/7 and isn't tied to a release time. This means that news can be covered at any time.
- **Shorter timelines** – With more pressure on journalists they often have shorter timelines, so accessibility and response times are key.

- **More news** – Journalists who previously wrote one article for a print paper now have to also write 3 – 5 articles for online editions. They have to create more news and are always on the lookout for relevant, interesting stories. This also means that they have to create MORE content, so the easier you can make it for them the better.
- **Smaller niche sites** – There are also many small, niche and community sites. While it used to be that big publications like the Wall Street Journal or USA Today were the holy grail of PR, now there are many smaller sites that may have a more relevant and engaged audience.
- **Contributing writers** – Many news sites now have contributing writers in addition to professional paid journalists. For example, many online versions of popular magazine like Inc and Fortune get most of their content from pre-selected industry-expert contributors.
- **Journalists are people too** – This isn't specific to digital (I suppose they were always people) but keep in mind that journalists are people too. They get inspired from what they see on Facebook. They use search engines to find answers and experts. They use online resources to support their stories.

The Digital Press Room

Make sure that your website has a "Press" section. Most journalists are on a tight timeline – they need immediate access to resources in order to cover your business or include you in articles.

Example:
To make it easier for journalists to include me as an expert and get what they need I setup www.KristaNeher.com/resources with all of the information they need easily available. This positions me as an expert and increases my professionalism

while saving me time. Consider creating similar resources for your business and key executives.

The press section of your website should contain the following:
- Copies of press releases
- Contact information for press
- Downloadable resources
- Bios and images of top executives

Power Tip:
Create a digital resources section to make it easier for people to find what they need. Include your logo, a short description of your business, and high-resolution images.

The Digital Press Release

Optimizing your press release for digital is also vital if you want to be covered by the media. More and more even traditional news sites are creating online articles as well as content that they can blast on social media. Giving journalists as much information as possible in the right format makes it easier for them to do their jobs.

If you want your press release to be ready to travel digitally, consider including the following links or content in addition to the traditional press release.

- Downloadable high-resolution images that are relevant to your press release
- Downloadable logo
- Infographics or visuals that explain the content
- A short video (under two minutes)
- Screenshots or demonstrations
- Short-format content (tweets, boiler plate company description, etc. that can easily be included)

As you write your press release for digital, also be sure to consider SEO best practices in the content. Press releases and news articles often appear towards the top of search results. To maximize your exposure, be sure that your press release includes the keywords and phrases that people are likely to be searching for related to your press release topic.

Power Tip:
Journalists often use search engines to research stories, for sources, and for additional information. Optimizing every aspect of your PR content can increase your probability of being found by them.

Gaining Press Mentions

Gaining press mentions in digital is similar to traditional but with digital there is more news on more sites – which means more opportunities!

Some of the best emerging opportunities to gain press mentions for your business include:

- **SEO** – Build an SEO strategy for your business that includes being found by journalists. This should go beyond your press releases and include your website and profiles of key executives.
- **Contributors** – There are now many contributors to well-known publications beyond just traditional journalists. Consider reaching out to authors who contribute articles or check your network to see if you know anyone. These contributors are often pitched less frequently vs. full-time journalists and may be more receptive.
- **Niche and Small Publications** – There are now TONS of niche and small publications that are looking for news to cover. Often part-time or unpaid contributors run them. These sites may not have the biggest audiences, but they can be accessible to target with your PR efforts.

- **Guest Posts** – Many publications accept guest contributions. Look for the guest contributor guidelines or sections of a website and pitch a story! Some require you to submit a full story – invest in writing an article and see if you can get it placed.
- **Bloggers** – In addition to formal news sites there are bloggers who specialize in all sorts of niches and topics. If there are bloggers who are relevant to you, don't hesitate to reach out to them. *Note: Bloggers are often influencers and may look for compensation in return for covering a business.*
- **Infographics and "News Assets"** – Many online publications are looking for content. Infographics or other assets that are in themselves news can be nice, easy posts for news sites or blogs. Create images, infographics and videos that can be shared and used on news sites as an article.
- **Studies and Research** – Conducting research is easier than ever before. With research capabilities in online survey tools like www.SurveyMonkey.com. Many businesses use research as a way to create press – especially by broadly sharing key findings and graphics (charts and images). This may be a considerable undertaking, but the results can be huge.

Example:
My company and myself have been featured in HUNDREDS of publications, including sites like the New York Times and CNNm as a result of being found in search engines. Consider your SEO strategy for your business and your top executives through the lens of journalists searching.

Big Idea:
It is still about relationships! Regardless of whether your aspirations are big established media sites or niche publications, relationships will get you further than anything else. Invest in building relationships that count.

Online Word-of-Mouth

Word-of-mouth is one of the most trusted and effective advertising channels, yet for many businesses it is an afterthought. Social media and digital present a tremendous opportunity to grow reach of word-of-mouth.

If I had a great (or terrible) experience with your business I would probably only tell a handful of people in real life. Each time I wanted to share the experience I would have to invest time to share the story. Online I can share my experience quickly with many people. Average people on most social networks have over 100 connections. This means that they can easily reach hundreds of people quickly with a single message.

There are a few different types of online word-of mouth that you can consider activating for your business.

Remember:
Word-of-mouth doesn't just happen. Regardless of the type of word-of-mouth you want to generate be sure that you have a specific strategy to implement it.

User-Generated Content

I could probably write an entire book just on this topic. User-generated content is when other people create and share content related to your business. There are many ways to encourage people to create content, below are the most effective strategies.

Create Sharable Moments or Experiences
One of the best ways to get people talking is to create things they want to talk about. Some think that if you have a great or interesting product that people will talk about it. The reality is that businesses deliberately create talkable experiences to drive word-of-mouth online.

I was recently in Russia and visited a craft cocktail bar that was extremely popular and had great reviews online, despite it being almost impossible to find. When they delivered drinks, they put them on wooden platters with dry ice smoking out to turn the drink into a moment that I shared on Instagram.

At our Boot Camp workshops we started giving attendees t-shirts because they love to take pictures in their Boot Camp Digital shirts! Consider how you can make your experiences more interesting and talkable to drive social media mentions.

 Netflix has a show called Stay Here where they help people improve their rental income from vacation rental properties like AirBnB. One of the things they do at each property is create an "Instagramable Moment." They create a setting that is designed for people to take pictures and share.

Promote a Hashtag or Your Username

Even if you have sharable experiences, you want to make sure that your business is mentioned when people share it.

For example, a friend recently posted a picture of a great meal he had in the restaurant. He talked about the dish but didn't mention the name of the restaurant. Hashtags are commonly used online to tag a business or conversation theme in a social media post. If the restaurant had promoted a hashtag or their username, perhaps my friend would have used them in his post and promoted the restaurant along with the food.

If and when you create talkable experiences or determine which parts of your business are most talkable, use a hashtag or share your username to encourage people to incorporate your business into the conversation.

Any business can create a hashtag that promotes their business. The hashtag should be short, clear, simple, and not already used. The bigger challenge is promoting and encouraging people to us it. Choose a hashtag and work on putting it in front of people at the right time in the right way when you have given them something to talk about (or there is inherently something to talk about) to drive social mentions of your business.

Contests or Promotions

Contests and promotions are great ways to get people talking and sharing content, especially when they are strategic and well executed. Contests can be a powerful and fun way to connect with your target audience and get them engaged with your business.

Many businesses use contests a few times a year to drive excitement and energize their audience. Many contest entries require sharing content online or voting, so they can also drive word-of-mouth.

Contests range from informal (eg. simple Facebook post that says comment for a chance to win), to semi-formal (eg. posters that offer a chance to win something for using a hashtag), to formal (eg. a photo contest with big-scale prizes and media promotion).

Power Tip:
There are rules and regulations around contests that you should be aware of. There are typically local laws that require disclosures when you run a contest. In addition, social networks like Facebook have guidelines about what you can and can't do. Check local laws and social network terms of service before creating an online contest.

Contests and promotions have declined in their popularity online over the last few years because they often resulted in low-quality interactions from people outside of the target audience. A restaurant ran a contest to win a gift card and over half of the entries were from outside of the state.

That being said, strategic contests can be fun and effective to grow your business. For example, a dog food company creating a dog photo contest could be a great way to build awareness with dog owners and give them a way to share their passion for their dogs. A door installation company did a contest to show your ugly door for a chance to win. These contests are strategic and appeal specifically to the target audience.

Too many contests can be a crutch for businesses to generate interest and engagements. For example, a restaurant ran weekly contests on their Facebook Page. After a few weeks the same 50 people were entering every contest. While they were getting a lot of engagements, they weren't ultimately achieving their business goal of boosting awareness since they were only appealing to the same people.

Big Idea:
Make sure that contests fit with your business strategy. Some businesses do giveaways to drive engagements on social media, but check that this matches your strategy. Monitor KPIs and participation to be sure that you are getting the results you want from your contest.

Digital contests are extremely easy to run. For example, a simple Facebook contest that uses comments and posts doesn't require any setup or technology. For more complex contests there are existing contest platforms which makes them easy to run.

Tool: Contests
Check out contest platforms like woobox.com that handle all aspects of running social contests for you. These tools can make it easy to run a formal contest.

Set KPIs or goals for your contest and measure how your contest performs relative to your business objectives. Start small, try one and judge success to see how it performs.

Remember:
In addition to setting up the contests you'll need a plan to drive people to enter the contest. Be sure that promoting the contest is a part of your strategy. Many businesses are disappointed by the number of entries in their contests because they didn't take the time to promote it effectively.

Create Shareable Content

Another key way to have your message spread is to create content that people want to share and talk about. In the early days of online marketing everyone wanted to create a "viral video." They've since realized that virality is extremely difficult to engineer, but focusing on interesting, relevant, and sharable content is a strategy that can get results.

People share content that they like or get value from online. On Pinterest 80% of the content is re-pinned – meaning people are sharing things that they love online.

Power Tip:
Be sure that your content is set up to suggest and encourage sharing. For example, include social sharing buttons on your website. Check how your content looks when shared on Facebook and LinkedIn. Make sure your videos are on sharable platforms like YouTube.

As you consider your content strategy – for your social networks, your blog, your website – evaluate whether or not you are creating sharable content.

Big Idea:
Test, learn, and experiment to determine how to best create content that people want to share. You may not have all the answers upfront, so try different things and relentlessly monitor your KPIs to learn and track the content that performs best.

Employee Advocacy

Employee advocacy can be a powerful way to grow your brand impression online. Each of your employees is connected to hundreds of business professionals. Plus your employees are trusted by their friends, family, and network making their recommendations or mentions even more valuable.

Employee advocacy focuses on encouraging and inspiring your employees to promote your business online. This usually is beneficial to both the business and the individual. Many businesses don't consider how their employees can be advocates for them, which is a big missed opportunity.

Power Tip:
It is common for employees to use a disclaimer when they promote their employer online. The reason is that the FTC requires people to disclose if they have a vested interest in a product or service that they promote. This is usually executed with a simple hashtag. For example, employees of Procter & Gamble use #pgemp when they promote P&G products online.

Benefits of Employee Advocacy

According to LinkedIn, companies that empower their employees to share content have better performance.

Companies who empower employees to share content perform better

They can more easily increase their reach and engagement, attract top talent and sell their products

58%	**2x**	**45%**
Talent	Marketing	Sales
Social enterprises are 58% more likely to attract top talent and 20% more likely to retain them	Content shared by employees has 2x higher engagement versus when shared by a company	Salespeople who regularly share content are 45% more likely to exceed quota

Each of your employees has a network of people who know, like and trust them. Each employee who shares your content could be reaching hundreds of people – multiply that by the number of employees you have.

Businesses harness the power of their employees in a number of ways:

- To promote job openings
- To build awareness
- To share thought-leadership and equity content that positions the business well
- To share PR mentions
- To share their social media posts
- To build awareness and action for new products or promotions
- Build awareness of product features and benefits
- Position employees as experts

These are only some of the ways that employees are used. This is a powerful strategy for both B2B and B2C businesses.

I recently gave a workshop to a sales team about how to become advocates for their employer online. At the end of the workshop employees had already generated more social reach and engagement for the posts than the employer had.

How to Encourage Employee Advocacy

The key to success is to inspire and motivate employees to share content and make it as easy as possible for them. Some employees will already naturally advocate for their employer, but many aren't sure what to post and are hesitant about what is or isn't appropriate.

It generally isn't a good idea to require or force employees to share content through social media. A better strategy is to appeal to the self-interest of employees – what is the benefit for them of sharing information about your business online.

Big Idea:
Conduct a workshop or training for employees on effective use of social media. This has the advantage of making sure employees understand what not to do online while also empowering them to advocate and share on behalf of the employer. We recently conducted a workshop where employees became advocates to promote the company in the industry – both for hiring and building awareness with prospective clients.

Start by determining the strategic objective you want to achieve as a result of your employee activism. Next give your employees a clear idea of their dos and don'ts and how they can support your business and themselves through social media. Finally, make it easy for them. Conduct a kick-off workshop, give them sample content, and show them examples of employees who are already doing a great job.

Tool: LinkedIn Elevate
LinkedIn Elevate is a tool created by LinkedIn to make it easier for employees to advocate for their employer and share business updates on their LinkedIn profiles. This makes it easier for business professionals to have a steady flow of thought-leadership status updates on their profiles, and also amplifies business messages.

Conversational Marketing

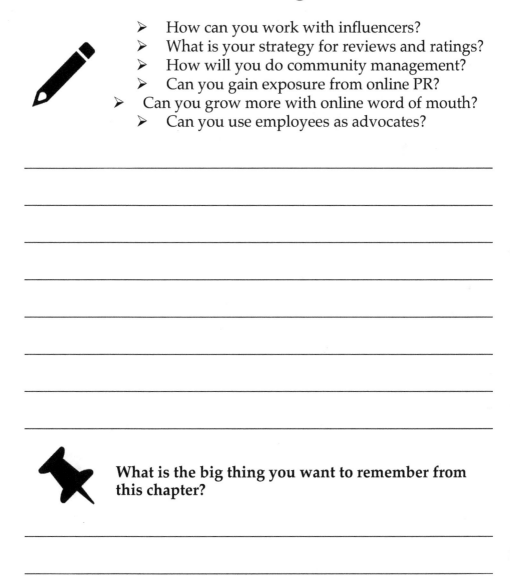

- ➢ How can you work with influencers?
- ➢ What is your strategy for reviews and ratings?
- ➢ How will you do community management?
- ➢ Can you gain exposure from online PR?
- ➢ Can you grow more with online word of mouth?
- ➢ Can you use employees as advocates?

_____

_____

_____

_____

_____

_____

_____

What is the big thing you want to remember from this chapter?

_____

_____

Go to www.ThatActuallyWorks.com/DigitalMarketing for your free action planner and bonus resources.

Chapter 11: Email Marketing

In a world distracted by social media and mobile, email is sometimes forgotten as a strategic digital communications channel. Email marketing continues to be one of the most effective digital marketing channels for businesses.

Emails are widely used by people, they are seen by people via their inbox, and they are effective at driving action. While social media posts and ads tend to be viewed more passively, emails are a medium that people actively engage with - if the emails are any good.

- 58% of adults **check** their email **first thing** in the **morning**.
- 64% of people say they **open** an email because of the **subject line**.
- 61% of consumers **like** to receive **weekly** promotional emails.
- 95% of online **consumers use email**.

Email Marketing Strategy

Email is a popular digital marketing tool because it reaches almost everyone, and it is effective at multiple marketing objectives. When marketers were asked about their objectives in using email as a part of their strategy, their top objectives were:

- 64% - Sell products and services
- 52% - Generate leads
- 51% - Drive website traffic
- 51% - Brand awareness
- 25% - Request a referral

As you can see, these objectives represent almost every stage of the marketing funnel.

Attract/Reach
- Educate them about your business/brand
- Share thought-leadership content to stay top-of-mind
- Welcome them to your community, group, etc.

Nurture
- Personalize your email content for your audience
- Build know, like + trust
- Share helpful, thought-leadership content to position your brand as an expert
- Help them make a decision by providing valuable information

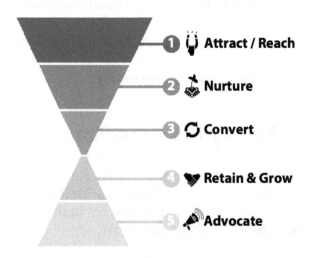

Convert
- Have a clear call-to-action
- Show clear benefit to reader – what's in it for them if they complete the action?

Retain & Grow
- Build loyalty by making them feel special/exclusive
- Be useful and relevant and create content that is a good fit for existing customers

Advocate
- Encourage shares with friends
- Encourage positive reviews

While email content and strategy can target every stage of the marketing funnel, it is usually not the best tool at truly generating new awareness. The reason is that you need email addresses to send emails to – and if you have their email they are already aware of you.

 Big Idea:
You can use email for every stage of the marketing funnel and many email strategies focus on achieving a combination of objectives. Make sure that each email has only one objective, but if you send multiple emails you may use them for multiple objectives.

Types of Email Marketing

Newsletters are the most popular form of email marketing, but they aren't the only one. There are three types of emails that you may consider in your email marketing execution – Newsletters, Autoresponders, and Personal.

Krista Neher

Newsletter Emails

Newsletter emails are the most common type of email. These are emails that are typically sent on a regular basis to a pre-defined list. Most businesses start with email newsletters to keep people up-to-date on their business and aware of incentives, new products, or sales. They are also used to establish thought-leadership and strengthen connections, especially by B2B companies.

Power Tip:
More advanced newsletter marketers (typically with large lists) will segment their lists, so different people get different emails. This could be based on product interest, previous email responses, or other factors. This usually leads to better results but is only appropriate if you have different types of people on your list that would respond better to different messages. For example, at Boot Camp Digital we have a corporate training newsletter and a digital marketer newsletter, since each of these groups is looking for different content.

Autoresponder Emails

Autoresponders are frequently used by B2B businesses but can be used for almost any type of business. Rather than sending the same email to your entire list on the same day, an autoresponder will send emails in a pre-defined sequence starting on day 0. The emails are "triggered" by an event or upon being added to the email list.

For example, if you fill out a form showing interest in attending one of our Boot Camps we'll send you a series of emails:
- Immediate – Thanks for your interest + brochure
- Day 4 – How can we help?
- Day 10 – Why our program is top rated.
- Day 14 – What is holding you back?

- Day 20 – Special offer
- Day 25 – Offer expires
- Day 30 – Parting thoughts

This is just an example, but you can see that we can create a strategic sequence of emails based on a trigger or starting point.

The advantage of this is that people receive a custom designed set of emails focused on driving action that initiates when they are most interested. The custom email path gets them the right email at the right time vs. a generic newsletter email.

Power Tip:
Most businesses use autoresponders in conjunction with email newsletters. Autoresponders can also be tracked, analyzed, an optimized over time.

Personal Emails

We are often so focused on our official email campaigns that we forget the power of personal messages. A personal request is the most effective way to drive action and can be particularly effective when you want to drive action from a small group of people, or people you have a relationship with.

For example, in requesting reviews, where you really need to generate a handful of reviews a week a personal email request will be more effective. Sometimes advocacy or referral campaigns can also work best when sent personally.

Power Tip:
In order to be compliant with email legislation (for example the CANSPAM Act in the US) email software should be used for any mass emails. Personal emails should be sent individually to people from your email.

Email Marketing Software

When sending emails most businesses use email software. Email software allows you to easily create professional emails and send them to large email lists automatically.

Email software platforms also make sure that your emails are compliant with any legal standards. For example, the CANSPAM Act in the US has guidelines for mass emails, including allowing people to opt-out and showing the address of the business in the email. Email software platforms incorporate this into the emails automatically.

When choosing an email service provider there are thousands of choices. It is important to think about the features and functions that you need from your email marketing tool. Different businesses will have different needs.

Consider the features you need from your email provider:
• Pre-made templates
• Coding required?
• Integration
• Segmentation and personalization
• A/B testing
• Reporting + Analytics
• Marketing Automation
• Price/List size
• Scalable
• Integration with other systems (for example CRM)

There are MANY email marketing platforms to choose from. Some of the most popular (in order from cheapest and easiest to start for small business to more enterprise appropriate) are:
• MailChimp
• Constant Contact

- Campaign Monitor
- iContact
- Infusionsoft
- AWeber
- Pardot

Power Tip:
If you want to start collecting email addresses but aren't ready to send emails, most platforms have a free account where you can easily get code to add an email form to your website. When you're ready, they'll be there.

---

3 Steps to Effective Email Marketing

Beyond having a clear defined strategy and execution plan, there are three main stages in email marketing success:
1) Collect email addresses
2) Drive opens of your emails
3) Generate action

Planning is the key to **success**. Your plan should focus on building an **audience**, creating great **content** that moves them to take an **action**, and **optimization** for maximum **results**.

Depending on where you are currently at you may choose to focus on a different stage. For businesses starting out it is best to focus on the steps sequentially.

Power Tip:
Even if you aren't ready to start sending emails, start collecting them! Let people sign up for your upcoming newsletter. This way when you launch your email efforts you will already have a list to market to!

Collect Email Addresses

In order to send emails you need to have addresses. Start collecting email addresses as soon as possible in as many places as possible. Over time your list will grow and email will become a more strategic part of your efforts.

Where to Ask for Emails

You can collect email addresses anywhere and everywhere. I've seen small businesses and retailers request email addresses in the checkout process, B2B companies get emails at trade shows, and email opt-in forms in almost EVERY digital channel.

The best way to approach collecting email addresses is to do a touchpoint analysis for your business. Consider all of the touchpoints that you have with prospects and customers (or whoever your target audience is) and evaluate each touchpoint as an opportunity to request email addresses.

Digital Marketing That Actually Works

Before purchase	During purchase	After purchase
Social media	Store or office	Billing
Ratings and reviews	Website	Transactional emails
Testimonials	Catalog	Marketing emails
Word of mouth	Promotions	Service and support teams
Community involvement	Staff or sales team	Online help center
Advertising	Phone system	Follow ups
Marketing/PR	Point of sale	Thank you cards

Some of the most common places to build your email list are:
- Website
- Lead ads
- Contests
- Checkout (in person and online)
- Social networks
- In-store
- Trade shows or events
- Networking events
- Business card drop contests

These are just a few ideas, and depending on your type of business you'll have different options that work best. The website is usually the top source for most businesses.

Power Tip:
You can buy email lists, but they usually aren't very effective. These lists can be expensive and the email addresses are also sold to many other companies. In addition, while **you** may be interested in sending your emails to this audience **they** may not be open to getting emails from you. Exercise caution in purchasing email addresses, as many businesses don't get great results.

Have a Value Proposition

When asking people to join an email list, make sure you offer a compelling reason. Here are some reasons that might encourage someone to share their email address:
- Get coupons
- Early access to a sale/new product
- Valuable or informational content
- Free resources
- Free anything
- Contest entry
- Birthday club
- Sneak peek at content
- Solve a specific problem for them

Power Tip:
Test, test, test. As you get started, test different calls-to-action and value propositions to get people to subscribe to your emails. Through testing you'll be able to find the most effective call-to-action.

Keep It Simple

Keep it as simple and ask for as little information as possible (unless you have a very high value incentive) to maximize your conversion rate. Also, don't ask for tons of information. It might be nice to know but you probably won't actually use anyway.

Business card drops at tradeshows and restaurants are popular because they are so easy.

Big Idea:
Keep in mind that requesting an email address or other information is a value exchange. People should be getting something of value from you in return for giving you their information. The more information you ask for, the more compelling your value proposition should be.

Get Your Emails Opened

It doesn't matter how many email addresses you have if people don't open your emails. Getting your emails opened comes down to two things: 1) Your subject line and 2) Your historical emails.

Subject Lines

Writing great subject lines is important and the biggest driver of whether or not people open your emails. While there are some best practices here, every business is different, and different things work for different audiences.

Some pro-tips for subject lines that work are:
- Short (<30 characters perform best)
- Grabs attention
- Personalized
- Avoid spammy words
- Don't mislead

When it comes to subject line angles that work, there are five things to think about. Remember the acronym CURVE.

Curiosity
- "Buffer has been hacked – here is what's going on", "DO NOT Commit These Instagram Atrocities"

Urgency
- "Save today only", "Where to drink beer right now"

Relevancy
- "You're missing out on points", "Top 3 baby formulas for healthy babies"

Value
- "Follow these 10 interview tips to get hired", "Everything you wanted to know about email copy but were too afraid to ask"

Emotion
- "Will you put down your phone to save a child's life?", "Boom shakalaka! Let's get started."

 Power Tip:
Don't mislead in your subject line just to drive opens. Keep in mind that you need people to not just open this email, but all of your emails. Be creative but not misleading.

Test Subject Lines

The best way to know what really works is to test, test, test. Test different subject lines to see what your audience responds best to.

Email subject lines can be tested. You can send a test to a small portion of your list to see which subject lines generates the most opens. The winner can be sent to the entire list. Additionally, many email software providers have A/B split testing built in to how they operate.

Retarget Non-Openers

Another strategy to improve open rates over time is to resend emails that haven't been opened with a new subject line.

For example, a business sent an email to their list and only 20% opened it after a week. So they sent the same email to the 80% who didn't open with a new subject line.

This strategy can lead to more email opens over time.

Manage Your Track Record

One of the factors that impact your email open rate is the previous emails that you've sent and how valuable they were to people. If someone opens an email and it isn't valuable to them they may unsubscribe, or they may just stop opening your emails.

Your historical emails play a big role in your open rates. Think of your own behavior – there are many emails you probably get but never open and others that you look forward to.

 Big Idea:
Track your analytics and look for negative feedback (unsubscribes, low clicks, low open rates) as these signal that your emails aren't adding value.

Drive Action from Your Emails

Even if people open your emails, you aren't done yet! You need to drive ACTION from them. Each email that you send should have a clear and single purpose. Sometimes with email newsletters we get so focused in the schedule, timing, and delivery method that we forget about what we want the email to actually do.

Business Objective

The first step to driving action from your emails is to have a clear and focused idea of what action you want to drive. Many emails start with a template and the business completes the template each month, often with 5 – 10 pieces of content. But what is the goal? What are they hoping to have happen?

Even if the action isn't clicking or buying, there should be a goal to specifically achieve something for your business. Start with a clear idea of what your email should do.

Power Tip:
Many emails become cluttered because they lack focus on a business objective. More content can be a distraction from what you really want. Less is more. Try to focus your email content as much as possible.

Structure

Determine the appropriate structure for your email based on what you want it to achieve. As more and more people view emails from their mobile phones simple formats are becoming favored. With less screen space, single focus, shorter content, less designed emails are becoming more popular and generating better results.

The first decision is the overall structure of your email. What content will you include in your and in what order?

The email should be structured to be short, with a single clear focus, easily scannable and with compelling copy at the beginning to draw people in.

Again, keep in mind your communication goal when choosing a structure, and eliminate content that doesn't add value.

Format

The format of your email refers to how your email will be laid out visually. That format should reflect your business objective.

Simpler formats are more and more popular because people are spending less time on a specific email (with mobile they have shorter sessions) and viewing emails on mobile devices (where they have smaller screens).

Also structure your format to be optimized for scanners. Many people don't read word-for-word content – they quickly scan to find what they are most interested in. Format so that your main points stand out. Use headers, bullets and buttons to draw attention to what matters most.

Content Ideas

Once you have the basic structure and format decided, consider the content that you actually want to share in the email. Many emails (especially email newsletters) contain A LOT of content.

Incorporate only the content that is connected to your business objective for the email. Eliminate content that may be a distraction.

Consider content that is both valuable to your business but also valuable or interesting to your audience.

Copy Tips

Copy matters. A lot. Craft compelling copy.

Think in terms of the reader. Use "you" language to speak directly to the reader with a clear value proposition.

Keep your call-to-action towards the top of the email and possibly repeat it towards the bottom.

Add personality and storytelling to build a connection with the reader. Your goal in copy is to draw someone in and inspire them to take action, or change their perception about something.

Images

Images are a part of most emails, although they are not required. The advantage of images is that they can add value and increase the branding + messaging of your emails. The right picture can be worth a thousand words.

If you use images, try to limit them to three or less and keep in mind that some email providers don't load images automatically. Make sure that your email works without the images and that your image is adding value.

Driving Action Overview

At the end of it all, the most important thing is that your email strategy grows your business and is valuable to your audience.

Evaluate your email through the lens of your audience. In just a few seconds, what would you take away from the email? Does that match your business goal? Does that add value to your reader?

 Power Tip:
Eliminate content from your email that doesn't add value. Often email templates have lots of "boxes" that we feel the need to fill. Content should guide what you include, not templates. Focus on the content that matters to you and is valuable to the audience and eliminate everything else – even if it is a part of a template.

How Often to Email

One of the most common questions with email marketing is when and how often to email. While you can find industry averages about email frequency and dates/times to send, the reality is that different audiences respond differently. For example, I happily open daily emails from a business expert that has great content, but I wouldn't want daily emails from a retailer. The point is – test what is best for you let that guide your decision.

Email Frequency

Most email newsletters start with a monthly frequency. Also, if you use autoresponders or have sales reps emailing, try to keep site of the total number of emails that you are sending to people.

To determine your email frequency, think about CAR:

Content
- How often do you have relevant content?
- What is realistic for you?
- How often do customers want to hear your messages?

Averages

- What is the average for the industry?
- What do most people expect?

Re-evaluate
- Test and learn

When to Send Emails

There are lots of ideas about when to send emails. Some suggest that emailing in the middle of the week is best because people are active at work but caught up from the weekend. Others suggest sending on Sunday because it is the date that the fewest emails are sent.

The best time to send emails depends on a variety of factors including:
- Your product and when it is relevant to people
- When your audience is receptive
- If it is personal or business
- When your audience is online
- When they have time or are less inundated

That being said, the best way to know when to send is to test, test, test. Evaluate your emails to determine when you get the best open rates.

Analyze Results

The only way to know how your emails are performing and to improve them is to analyze your results and optimize based on what you find. Too often we put marketing on autopilot and don't spend the time to check if what we are doing really works; or invest some effort to determine if we could do it better.

Build analysis in to your plan for emails. Prior to sending an email just take a few minutes to look at previous email performance to understand what worked and what didn't work.

Most businesses look at a handful of key metrics to assess the performance of their emails:

- Open rate – the percent of people who opened the email.
- Click rate – the percent of people who opened and then clicked on something in the email. You may also look at clicks on specific links or calls-to-action.
- Negative feedback – unsubscribes or your email marked as "spam" is considered negative feedback. Most emails generate some negative feedback but look for trends (above or below) your normal rate.

When it comes to metrics, marketers always want to know what is a "good" open rate or click rate. While there are averages that exist, the most important thing is that yours is improving.

Big Idea:
Instead of focusing on benchmarks or industry averages, aim to improve. There are many factors that lead in to your results, and it is often unproductive to aim for an industry benchmark that is well below (or above) your current performance. Aim to improve.

Email Marketing

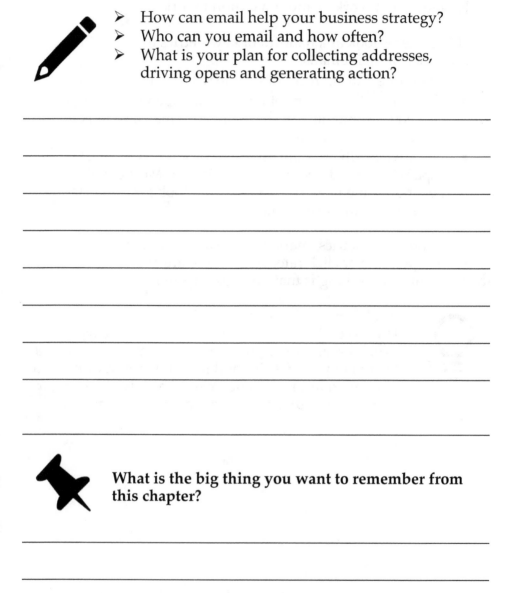

- ➢ How can email help your business strategy?
- ➢ Who can you email and how often?
- ➢ What is your plan for collecting addresses, driving opens and generating action?

_____

_____

_____

_____

_____

_____

_____

_____

What is the big thing you want to remember from this chapter?

_____

_____

Go to www.ThatActuallyWorks.com/DigitalMarketing for your free action planner and bonus resources.

Chapter 12: CRM

CRM stands for Customer Relationship Manager and it is a platform or system used by a company to manage all of their interactions and their relationship with a customer.

A CRM is generally used as a single source of information on a given customer. For example, in the Boot Camp Digital CRM we can see all of the information about a customer or prospect in one place. Email history, sales calls, products purchased, customer service, and all information we have on the person is tracked in a single system. This type of system allows us to effectively manage and improve the relationships we have with a customer or prospect.

The CRM information can also be used for targeting advertising. By connecting CRM data to an advertising platform like Facebook or Google businesses can send targeted ads to people in their CRM system.

Historically CRMs were primarily used for B2B businesses – as a way to track and store information on customers and prospects in a single place. Today they are used by many businesses to track customer and prospect records and as a single data source.

Why Businesses Use CRMs

A CRM has two major benefits: Efficiency (save time with everything in one place) and effectiveness (deal with customers more effectively by having all of their information in one place).

CRMs typically perform a variety of tasks:
- Contact Management
- Sales Lead Management
- Email Integration
- Marketing Automation
- Internal Team Sharing

CRM systems now interact with other systems and tools that provide even more functionality. For example, billing, surveys, accounting, and even marketing services can be connected to the CRM.

What Types of Businesses Use CRMs?

While this may seem like something that is only relevant for big companies or sales teams, CRMs can also be valuable to small and medium businesses. They can combine sales, email, and customer service data as well as keep all information in one place.

CRM systems can cost as little as under $100 a month to tens of thousands (or more) per month depending on how you use it and how many contacts you have. Salesforce is the most popular enterprise CRM and there are many popular small and medium business systems.

CRMs are mostly used for B2B sales, for higher-ticket purchases with longer buying cycles, or for purchases where the customer is known. For example, a car dealership could use a CRM to track and follow up with prospects who come and test drive cars. Since a purchaser may interact with multiple sales reps this allows the dealership to seamlessly interact and follow up with the prospect – without just relying on a single sales rep to manage everything. A retailer would probably use a CRM to track customers through their loyalty program or ecommerce.

Marketing Automation

Marketing automation runs with a CRM system to automate the process after a lead is collected or after an action is taken. Automation does what it sounds like – it automates follow-ups to drive consistency.

Marketing automation uses the CRM (and is often integrated into the CRM) to create a flow of interactions for a contact. For example, once a new sales lead enters my CRM, the system may assign the lead to a sales rep, and the marketing automation system could begin to trigger emails and phone call reminders for the sales rep.

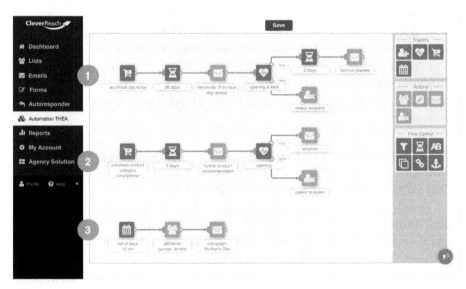

Marketing automation is a way to systematize your sales and communication processes, so that each contact receives the same communications (emails, phone calls, texts) at the same time based on the ideal path to drive conversions.

This is especially helpful, as sales reps don't always follow a set follow-up process. By systematizing the follow-ups, the process becomes more efficient and more consistent.

Big Idea:
Marketing automation can be powerful for any time businesses have leads but don't consistently follow up. Many businesses use this for after a trade show or for longer sales cycle processes (real estate, cars, etc.) to consistently send messages over time.

Inbound Marketing: The Connected CRM Strategy

Inbound marketing is a technique for drawing customers to products and services through online content marketing, social media marketing, search engine optimization, and branding. It is a strategy that uses "pull marketing" to attract clients to you. It is designed to bring qualified leads to your business and convert them over time.

Rather than pushing your message at people – through outbound sales teams or advertising – you create content and employ a digital strategy that attracts prospects to you.

Most businesses use a strategy of creating great content on their website with strong lead generation built in. The content is promoted through digital channels to attract people to it. Once they provide their information, they follow-up via CRM and marketing automation pushes them to become a customer.

The 3 Stages of Inbound Marketing

HubSpot has distilled the process of inbound marketing down to Attract, Engage, and Delight.

Attract is what draws prospects in to your business, and this could be paid or organic. A strong attract strategy brings the highest qualified leads to you.

The engage tools create a relationship by getting the right message to the right person at the right time. The main objective of engage is to draw them in to engage so you can capture their information and continue to communicate with them.

Finally, in the delight stage the emphasis is on automation and sales teams to deliver the right information to inspire them to actually do business with you.

Attract Tools	Engage Tools	Delight Tools
Ads	Lead Flows	Smart Content
Video	Email Marketing	Email Marketing
Blogging	Lead Management	Conversations Inbox
Social Media	Conversational Bots	Attribution Reporting
Content Strategy	Marketing Automation	Marketing Automation

Implementing Inbound Marketing

Successfully implementing inbound marketing requires seamlessly connecting multiple parts of the marketing funnel. While not technically complex, executing each area with excellence is challenging for many businesses. Many businesses invest in inbound marketing software but ultimately struggle to effectively implement across the three stages.

Power Tip:
Before investing in CRM or inbound marketing software nail some of the basic elements required for success. Build a solid content and lead generation strategy prior to tackling the post-lead conversion process.

Many CRM systems have features built-in to support inbound marketing, but there are also tools built specifically for this purpose. HubSpot and Marketo are two of the most popular inbound marketing platforms for small and medium businesses especially.

Remember:
Before jumping in to any system (CRM or marketing automation) make sure that you have the resources to execute well. Many businesses jump in with the best intentions but find that they have an expensive tool that they don't use.

CRM

- ➤ Can you use a CRM to grow your business?
- ➤ How will you find contacts to add to your CRM?
- ➤ How will you communicate to contacts to drive more conversions?

_____

_____

_____

_____

_____

_____

_____

What is the big thing you want to remember from this chapter?

_____

_____

Go to www.ThatActuallyWorks.com/DigitalMarketing for your free action planner and bonus resources.

Chapter 13: Mobile

Mobile marketing used to be considered a separate channel – similar to email or a website. Now over 50% of digital content is consumed via mobile devices. Email, websites, social and ads are all viewed more on mobile devices vs. desktop computers.

As a result, mobile optimization is now a part of any digital strategy or channel execution. In fact, we are switching from mobile optimization – where we create for desktop and optimize for mobile – to mobile first design. Digital executions are designed for mobile.

In addition to optimizing or better, designing digital for mobile, there are a few mobile first executions that apply specifically to mobile phones.

Mobile apps continue to be a way for businesses to offer relevant services to their customers. Apps are created for entertainment, socializing, and utility.

Messaging through platforms like Facebook Messenger and WhatsApp are outgrowing social networks and represent huge opportunities for marketers. Chatbots and AI (artificial intelligence) are transforming how businesses can communicate with their customers on mobile.

Regardless of how you proceed in mobile, be sure to start with the customer and their experience vs. starting with the technology.

Marketers sometimes get excited about new technology even though they don't have a strong value proposition for their customers or audience. This leads to money invested with little to no return.

Start with the consumer value proposition. What is in it for them? Why would they use this? Are they asking for this? How does it help them? What problems does it solve? Does it make their life better in some way?

Mobile Design and Optimization

Digital marketers used to talk about mobile optimization, which meant taking your existing desktop-based digital and making it work on mobile, to mobile first design, which is about designing for mobile.

Big Idea:
The reason mobile first is a challenge is because most marketers work on computers – so this is how digital marketing is evaluated. Evaluate digital creative on your phone, not your computer.

Designing for mobile means that your start your digital projects focused on mobile first. There are some specific consumption habits that makes mobile different vs. desktop that you should account for in your designs.

- **Smaller screens** – This should come as no surprise, but with smaller screen real estate you need simpler and less complicated designs that are easy to see and read on a mobile device.
  Keep things SIMPLE and CLEAN with less complex designs and shorter content.

- **Speed of the feed** – People move more quickly through content on mobile devices. Facebook, for example, shows significantly faster scrolling through mobile feeds vs. desktop.
  Get to the point fast and organize for scanning. Have ONE SINGLE focus and eliminate unnecessary details.

- **Shorter sessions** – On mobile people typically have shorter sessions. They are on and off devices 80 times a day on average, but for less time each session. Let that sink in for a second – 80 times a day on average.
  Make your message bite-sized so your main point is transmitted instantly.

- **Clicking with hands** – In order to facilitate mobile users who click with their hands, make sure that your content is well spread out and clickable links are not too close to each other.
  Check that your content can be clicked on and works well on mobile screens.

- **Mobile calls-to-action** – With mobile, people can click and open maps, initiate a phone call, or start to send an email.
  Incorporate mobile calls-to-action and mobile functionality into your content.

Mobile Apps

In the earlier days of digital marketing businesses were flocking to create their own mobile apps. Since then a few realities have slowed the business interest in them:

- Getting people to download your app is a challenge.
- Driving usage of an app is difficult.
- Creating for multiple devices is expensive.
- Maintaining apps is an ongoing investment over time.

- Customer support and servicing is often underestimated.
- The marketplace has become very competitive with many apps in most categories.

As a result of the above, many businesses had invested in apps and found that they weren't generating enough usage to justify a positive ROI.

At this point, there are five main strategies used by businesses with respect to mobile apps: Focus on Mobile Website, Create Your Own App, Build or Customize on an App Platform, Partner with Existing Apps, and Create Content on Existing Apps.

Focus on Mobile Website

Part of the decline in interest in mobile applications has come from the rise of use of the mobile web. Websites are now designed for mobile first, and many websites offer an excellent solution for mobile users.

When apps initially became popular, websites were designed for desktop and optimized for mobile. Plus, mobile web functionality wasn't as developed as it is now.

Every business should have a website that works well on mobile, but more and more your mobile site can do everything that an app would do.

As mobile internet speeds are faster, and people are more used to using mobile browsers, attention has shifted from customized applications to mobile websites.

Create Your Own App

Some businesses still create their own apps. For example, most banks, retailers, large loyalty programs, and software services have mobile applications.

Creating an app is still a viable strategy if you can provide a meaningful or necessary service to your customers through an application. Many applications are designed to be easier and better at performing routine functions vs. a website and provide a better user experience.

If you are thinking about creating your own application start with the customer – what is the customer benefit? Is it something customers ask for?

Build or Customize on an App Platform

Rather than creating your own application you can consider if an existing platform can create the functionality that you need. There are often existing platforms or technologies for most basic applications that businesses may want to run through mobile apps.

There are app platforms that exist where businesses can just add their content to quickly create their own application. For example, if you are a fitness instructor and want your own app, there are fitness instructor apps where you can pay a monthly fee to create one. Are you an expert with content you want to share with your fans? There are apps that you can easily create to connect with your content. Need an app for your loyalty program? There are apps that connect with popular loyalty programs to give you a standalone app quickly.

If your app doesn't have too much customization required, you can probably find an app platform that allows you to quickly create one from a template.

The advantage of these app platforms is that you can get started quickly with minimal investment. The downside is that you have to work within their templates and functionality. Even if an app platform can't do everything you want it is usually a good starting point. Once your app has traction you can invest more to make it more customized.

Partner with Existing Apps

Businesses that don't have the capacity or interest in creating their own app can partner with or sponsor existing applications.

Years ago, Charmin Toilet Paper found an existing application called "Sit or Squat" that helped people to find public restrooms and also included ratings and even photos. Rather than building their own app, Charmin sponsored the existing app and integrated their brand throughout it.

If you think you may want to create an app, check first that you have a unique idea. Don't build what you can borrow. Many businesses that have an app idea quickly find that one already exists. Rather than recreating something, allow someone else to deal with the complexity of creating and updating the app while you take advantage of the visibility.

Create Content on Existing Apps

In many industries and categories there are already plenty of applications that exist that consumers use to find aggregated information.

For example, in looking for restaurants people often use Open Table, Yelp, or Trip Advisor to make their decision. If you own a restaurant part of your strategy should be to manage and optimize your presence on these applications.

Check for the apps already used in your industry, and see if there is a way for your business to be integrated or present.

Messaging + Chatbots

Messaging platforms are becoming more and more popular with people and marketers. As early as 2015 top messaging platforms already had more users than top social networks. Messaging continues to grow with Facebook owning the top two (non-China) messaging apps – Facebook Messenger and WhatsApp.

Messaging apps usage is expected to continue to grow significantly and many expect that messaging will overtake phone numbers as a primary way that people communicate. For many messaging is more convenient as it is easy to share text, video, and images or have multi-person group video chats.

Despite the size of messaging apps, businesses have been slow to take advantage of them. This is in part because messaging applications are only just starting to roll out features for businesses to use them effectively. For example, WhatsApp only recently launched business profiles and Messenger is more proactively building and promoting business features.

The Advantages of Messaging

Messenger is a powerful platform for businesses for a few reasons:
1) **It is where people are** – People are already spending their time in Messenger, and as younger people prefer non-traditional channels, Messaging apps will continue to increase in importance.
2) **It is mobile first** – As mobile is more and more important businesses need to have an easy way to connect with customers on mobile.

3) **It is like an app in a platform** – With Messenger businesses can basically build applications directly in it. For example, if my bank offered it I could check my bank balance or transfer funds through Messenger.
4) **Natural language conversations** – With Messenger (even with bots) people can have natural language conversations. For example, instead of logging in to a website or app, I can just ask what my balance is, how far away my taxi is, or my flight status.
5) **The power of AI (artificial intelligence)** – Chatbots bring the power of AI to messaging. With this, businesses can anticipate your needs to provide superior service.
6) **Speak to a Human?** – Despite all of the technology, often people want to speak to a real, live human, and more and more that happens on Messenger.
7) **Subscriptions and push** – One of the reasons businesses LOVE Messenger is because they can have people subscribe and push them messages. Messenger messages have a high open rate and show up as a notification on most phones. This may change as more businesses adopt the channel, but at the moment businesses can get a lot of visibility.

The power of messaging apps is huge. In China, where messaging apps are more popular people use them to order and pay for taxis, to pay their bill at a restaurant, and to get ads from businesses.

How Businesses Use Messaging

Businesses use messaging platforms in a few different ways. This will continue to evolve as the platform becomes more robust.

- **Live chat** – Some businesses use Messenger as a way to speak to a human, similar to live chat on a website. It is important for businesses to manage expectations of response times. Facebook has a variety of tools to make it easy for businesses to use Messenger for customer service.

- **Voice calls** – WhatsApp allows texts, voice, and video calls, so many businesses use it as their main voice line. If you travel in Asia you'll see WhatsApp numbers promoted on everything from tour groups to restaurants. The flexibility of text and voice makes it appealing.
- **Mass messaging** – Businesses that have embraced chat are starting to use it to send mass messages to people. In this way it is used almost as email.
- **Functions of a mobile app** – Chat (through bots) gives businesses the ability to provide many different robust features through messaging. Businesses can create services for clients through Messenger.

As you can see, Messenger provides the functionality of multiple different services all in one. This is what makes it so powerful.

Chatbots

Chatbots are emerging as a key way for businesses to use the power of chat to automate business processes or services. They simulate a human conversation with back and forth messages but also offer advanced capabilities like artificial intelligence or connecting to other platforms.

chat·bot

/ˈCHatbät/ ◁)

noun

a computer program designed to simulate conversation with human users, especially over the Internet.

"chatbots often treat conversations like they're a game of tennis: talk, reply, talk, reply"

Businesses use chatbots to provide a variety of services for customers.

- **Customer service bots** – resolve common issues or connect you with a person.

- **Product recommendation bots** – Recommend a product based on your needs or an assessment.
- **Appointment bots** – Book an appointment for you.
- **Service bots** – Provide a service to the customer. This could be anything from helping to find an outfit to finding the best restaurant nearby.
- **Connected bots** – Bots can connect to other systems to give updates instead of having someone log in. For example, airlines have bots to send flight info and updates or loyalty programs can give you your balance or award you points.

These are only some of the things that bots can do. It can be easy or difficult to create a bot depending on the functionality you want. There are chatbot software solutions that are free or under $100/month that allow you to create basic bots from a template. These are easy to execute, but usually somewhat limited in functionality. MobileMonkey, Chatfuel and ManyChat are among the market leaders in this space.

A custom bot that connects with internal systems or is specific to your business can also be created, but requires more time and investment. These can cost anywhere from $20k - $250K depending on the functionality.

Big Idea:
If you are thinking about using chatbots, be sure that you have a strong consumer value proposition first. Start with the **customer** not the **technology.** Be sure you are solving a problem, offering a solution or providing a service to your customers.

Mobile Marketing

- ➢ Is all of your marketing optimized for mobile?
- ➢ Do you have any unique mobile opportunities? Voice? Text? Apps?
- ➢ Can you use messenger and Chatbots as a part of your strategy?

_____

_____

_____

_____

_____

_____

_____

What is the big thing you want to remember from this chapter?

_____

_____

Go to www.ThatActuallyWorks.com/DigitalMarketing for your free action planner and bonus resources.

PART 3: DIGITAL MARKETING MEASUREMENT

Measurement is one of the biggest challenges that marketers have when it comes to digital. This is somewhat surprising since in digital marketing we have more information and metrics than in almost any other marketing channel.

The problem is that we have lots of information and data but few insights. The key is analysis and understanding to drive action.

Many large organizations are actually reducing the number of metrics that they track. The reason is that by looking at too many things they are losing focus on what really matters to drive their business.

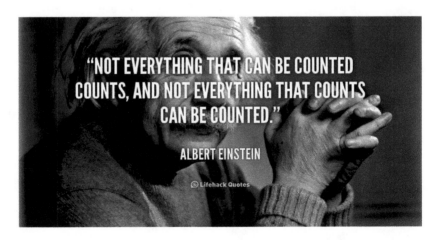

Measurement is a big topic and with so much data it can seem overwhelming. In this section we'll share how to make sense of the data and use it strategically to drive your business.

Chapter 14: Digital Marketing Measurement

Digital marketing measurement can be one of the biggest challenges. With so much to measure, how do you focus on what matters?

There are four steps to effectively measuring your digital marketing efforts: Start with Strategy, Set KPIs, Benchmark, and Report Regularly.

Start with Strategy

Strong measurement starts with strategy. If you don't know what you want to achieve you can't measure what matters. Your strategy should guide your metrics.

For example, even with a Facebook execution, your metrics and KPIs will be different depending on your objective. Your execution and metrics should line up based on your strategy and what you want to achieve for your business.

Even in evaluating an ad report, if you don't have a clear idea of the objective for the ad you can't judge success. For example, in the chart below a different ad would be more effective depending on your objective.

Campaign	Clicks	Reach	Cost per Click	Cost per Impression
Ad 1	3	35,752	$6.60	$0.51
Ad 2	167	6,329	$0.12	$2.66
Ad 3	86	5,514	$0.22	$3.18

In the example above if the goal was reach or brand awareness the first ad would be most effective. If the goal was driving traffic Ad 2 was most effective. The KPIs and metrics depend on the objective.

The same is true when evaluating content. When looking at a post or evaluating agency creative, the question isn't if it is "good" the question is if it is effective. For example, in judging the posts below there are many opinions about how they look, but without knowing the objective it is impossible to know if the content is effective.

If you've been following the book and action planner, you have already defined your goal, strategy, objective, and tactic. Your measurement plan will be set at the tactic level. For each tactic you should have a clear KPI and measurements that measure your success.

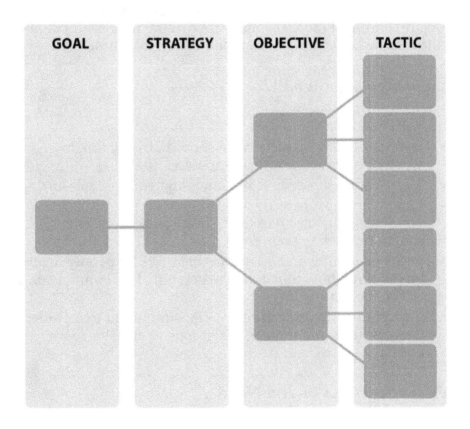

Setting KPIs

KPIs are commonly used to judge performance in digital marketing (and in other marketing as well). KPI stands for Key Performance Indicator. The idea is that since you typically can't measure your end goal (sales, donations, etc.) and specifically attribute them to one activity, you use a KPI which is a metric that indicates whether or not your efforts are achieving your goals.

The idea is if I can't directly measure sales or new clients, I want to track the things that suggest that I am getting sales or new clients. For example, people in my target audience reading my blog and signing up for email indicates that I am driving interested people to my site which should lead to sales and clients over time.

What makes a good KPI?

A strong KPI should:
- Be specific to your success – it should directly link to whether or not your efforts are successful.
- Measurable – It needs to be something you can measure.
- Link to business objectives – it should clearly tie back to your business objectives (and your business objectives should tie back to your goal)
- Focus on quality and quantity – many KPIs are only focused on quantity (how much did we get) but also should focus on the quality and value.
- Incorporate costs or efficiency – it is important to consider the cost (time and money) that it took to achieve your objective.

The 3 Types of KPIs You Need

To really understand if your marketing is effective you'll want to be sure that your KPIs measure quantity, quality, and cost. This gives you a full picture of your performance. You may be able to create a single metric that incorporates all of these, but often it takes two KPIs to incorporate quality, quantity, and cost.

Quantity – How much am I getting?
- The amount of the result that you are generating (eg. traffic, traffic growth, clicks, reach, impressions

Quality – How good is what I'm getting?
- The effectiveness of the result or the quality of the result (eg. conversions, time on site, awareness growth)

Cost – How cost effective is it?
- The cost per result or per quality to determine cost effectiveness
- Based on metrics/KPIs that matter for your business

Big Idea:
You may not be able to incorporate cost, quality, and quantity into a few KPIs. If not, get as close as possible.

Setting KPIs

Each tactic should have 1 -2 KPIs. Prioritizing a few KPIs doesn't mean that you should never look at other metrics, especially if you are evaluating performance. It means that you set a clear view of what you want to achieve and have selected a few metrics that best indicate if you are getting what you want.

In earlier days of digital, many businesses focused on metrics that didn't really matter for their business success. For example, many businesses focused on the number of fans they acquired on Facebook. While fan growth is a sign of a healthy Facebook Page, it should never have been their KPI or the main thing they wanted to achieve. In many cases they actually wanted reach – so reach (the number of people that saw their messages) should have been the KPI instead of fans.

You Get What You Measure

Keep in mind you typically get what you ask for and what you measure.

In the example above when social media managers were judged by their ability to get fans they focused their efforts on growing fans – even if those fans were not relevant to the business goals. Businesses purchased fans online or focused on contests to get more fans – even if the fans were not interested in the business.

When setting digital ads the ad delivery is always optimized to give you what you ask for. The same ad will generate more clicks if you ask for clicks or more reach if you ask for reach. Even with the exact same ad.

Remember:
Set KPIs that are strongly linked to your business objectives to be sure that you are measuring what matters most.

Benchmark

A benchmark is a way to understand if your digital marketing is performing well relative to a set standard or benchmark. For example, you may have an open rate on your email of 10% - is this good? Should you be satisfied? What does good look like in digital marketing?

Benchmarks are helpful to answer the question of whether or not we are doing well with our digital marketing efforts.

Example:
In evaluating content for an agency, we were able to identify the content that performed best. However, when looking at benchmarks from Facebook it all performed well below benchmarks set by Facebook and standard for the industry. Rather than setting a goal of incremental performance the agency realized that they needed to change their approach overall

since while some content did better, it all did poorly on a more objective scale.

Benchmarking answers this question. It tells us if we are hitting an objective standard with our results. You may use a benchmark to evaluate your KPI performance or for other metrics that you evaluate.

While benchmarking sounds like an easy concept it is more challenging once you start trying to set them.

Setting a Strong Benchmark - IAP

While it can be tempting to set a benchmark based only on industry averages (for example aiming for a click-through-rate that matches industry standards) it is important to keep in mind that based on your unique business, marketing objectives, and investment you may see valid differences.

Improvement
The most important thing (even if you are well below or above industry averages) is that you are improving. Always aim for improvement that is realistic for your business.

Averages
Most businesses set benchmarks based on industry averages. While this should be a part of your strategy, it should not be the only think you look at.

WATCHOUT: These are averages and may not be representative of your industry or approach.

There are three types of benchmarks that you can consider:
- Industry averages
- Internal Benchmarks - other brands/businesses
- External Benchmarks – agency partners in your industry

Plan
Finally, check that your benchmark is realistic based on your time and resource investment. If you have a large investment it is reasonable to expect more than if you have a small investment. It is also helpful to check that your benchmark or goal is aggressive enough to generate a positive return on investment.

What Makes a Good Benchmark?
- Realistic
- Improvement vs. history
- Represents real success
- Linked to your investment

Power Tip:
When setting benchmarks it is also a good idea to consider your benchmark relative to your investment. For example, if you are making a big investment for minimal growth is it worth it?

Report Regularly

Regular reporting is an important part of your measurement plan. Be sure that your report drives the focus towards the KPIs that matter most, but also include measurements and other information to show why.

Most businesses report on a monthly basis, but based on your investment you may want weekly or quarterly reports.

Creating Impactful Reports

Consider Your Audience
Creating a report for a marketing director should be different than a CEO. Different levels in an organization need different levels of

detail. Know your audience and, if needed, ask them what they want to best understand from the report.

Know WHY You Are Reporting

This may seem obvious – you are reporting to understand how your investment is performing. At a high level this is true, but different audiences may want to understand different things from the reports. Understand what you audience wants to learn as a result of the report.

Eliminate Unneeded Details

Often reports include way too much content. Many reports include every number available. Most of these metrics aren't important and also don't change over time. For example, the demographic composition of your social media following isn't likely to change each month, so it doesn't need to be included in a monthly report.

Focus on What Matters

Focus on what matters most and include the KPIs on a cover page on the front. You may include numbers beyond your most important KPIs but design your report to drive the focus to the numbers that really matters.

Provide Context

It is helpful to provide context to numbers where you can. This means share the target or benchmark or the percentage increase/decrease vs. the previous month or year. Provide details with the numbers that add context to what they mean. Standalone numbers are difficult to derive meaning from.

Share Insights

A good report shouldn't just include numbers – it should give insights. Share some details about how things are going and why. This is what really matters – the analysis and insights about the performance.

Include Qualitative
Where appropriate include qualitative examples. For example, sharing that you generated five new reviews isn't always as impactful as showing the actual reviews. Show the impact with qualitative information.

Reporting Tools

Rather than spending hours creating reports each month, there are many digital marketing management tools that will create reports for you.

Big Idea:
Consider how much time you spend creating reports and ask if it is worth it to invest in a tool that includes reporting. The reports from digital management tools often look better than manual reports and save lots of time.

Most tools have free trials so you can test some out and see which ones work best for your business. Be sure that the metrics that matter to you are included in the report.

Tool: Google Data Studio
Google has a free tool called Google Data Studio that will incorporate data from multiple sources and display it in visual formats (graphs, charts, etc.) in one place. You can create a custom report with the data represented in a way that is useful to you and easily populate it on demand at the click of a button.

Digital Marketing Measurement

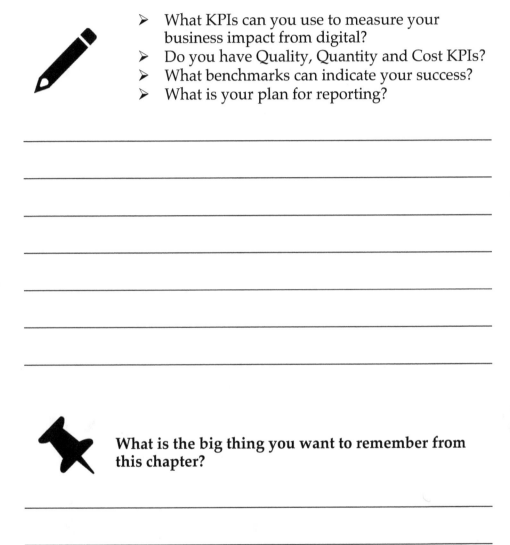

> ➢ What KPIs can you use to measure your business impact from digital?
> ➢ Do you have Quality, Quantity and Cost KPIs?
> ➢ What benchmarks can indicate your success?
> ➢ What is your plan for reporting?

_____

_____

_____

_____

_____

_____

What is the big thing you want to remember from this chapter?

_____

_____

Go to www.ThatActuallyWorks.com/DigitalMarketing for your free action planner and bonus resources.

Chapter 15: Analytics & Optimization

Analysis goes beyond KPIs and just the numbers – analysis is about weeding through the numbers to understand WHY. In order to effectively analyze performance you'll need to have business understanding as well as know about the digital executions.

The numbers will never tell the full story. They tell the what – the analysis tells the so what – why does this matter? What is causing this?

Once you've analyzed the data, optimization is the next step. Based on what you learned, what will you do differently? How will you improve or optimize your efforts?

Analytics Framework

The purpose of analytics is to go beyond the numbers and offer an explanation based on insights. Reporting or KPIs alone aren't enough to paint a picture. The question is what is causing the numbers and what should we do about it.

To facilitate strong analytics (or if you are on the receiving side of reports) challenge yourself to ask:

What – The data
So What – The insight
Now What – The action

This is the framework we'll use in this chapter to move from data and information to analysis and insights.

What –The Data

The first step of analytics is the WHAT. You need to understand what the data is telling you. While this sounds simple often it isn't. Many of the brand managers look at reports from agencies every month and have no real idea what the report is telling them.

The first step is understanding the data. To understand the data, you'll need to:
1) Understand the metric and what it means.
2) Know what drives the metric – what could cause it to go up or down?
3) Gain context for the numbers you are looking at – are they going up or down? Are they above or below benchmark?
4) Determine what the numbers are telling you.

Power Tip:
Most analytics tools or insights on websites will explain terms if you hover your cursor over the term. Familiarize yourself with the key terms and what they mean.

So What –The Insight

Once you know what the data is telling you, the next step is to figure out so what – what does this MEAN?

The goal of the **So What** or insight is to develop understanding from the numbers, or the WHY.

Once you know what the numbers are telling you, determine why they are what they are. In order to develop insights, you'll often need to look at multiple numbers together to see the full picture of what is happening.

You may be able to develop insights just from the data, but it is helpful to have more business context.

1) Did anything out of the ordinary happen with the business that month?
2) What did the digital execution look like on that channel? Did anything change in the execution or investment?
3) What other metrics are linked to the one you are analyzing? What else should you look at?
4) What is the data telling you? Why is the number what it is? Is it good or bad? What caused it?

Developing insights is often a challenge, as you need to understand the numbers and be able to figure out what they mean. Strong insights answer the question of "So What?" or "Why"?

Power Tip: Storytelling
Think of the **So What** as storytelling. What is the story behind the data that explains it? Try to turn your insights into a story that you can explain to others.

Now What –The Action

The last step in analytics is **Now What**. What is the action we should take as a result of the insight? What should we do?

A lot of analysis stops at **What** and very few go to the level of **Now What**. This is arguably the most important part. Looking at reports but doing nothing isn't particularly valuable and doesn't actually add business value or impact.

Acting on insights is how you deliver impact and drive a business.

Based on the analysis what steps should we take? How do we further improve performance? What should we avoid? How can we better use our resources?

The **Now What** step can also be considered the optimization step. Optimization is about making changes and improvements to your executions to get better results over time. Even if your results are good you should always be optimizing and improving your efforts.

What, So What, Now What Examples

To help bring this concept to life let's explore some examples. Since we don't know the business context of digital execution we've taken some liberties with the insights.

Example: Google Analytics

What: I grew more users (12%)

So What: New users were primarily from social media as we promoted our content more. While users grew, our QUALITY of traffic dropped with a higher bounce rate and less time on site.

Now What: People are coming to our site to view blog posts but not staying. We should test conversion methods (webinar, suggested content) to get more from our visitors.

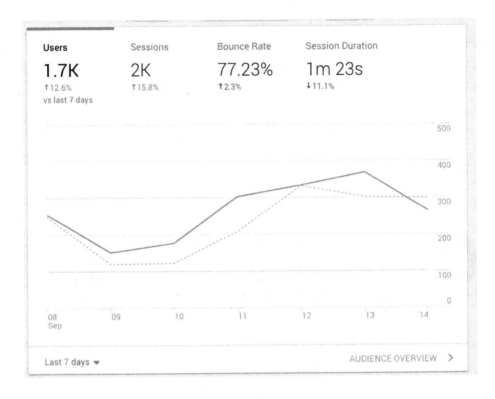

Users   Sessions   Bounce Rate   Session Duration

1.7K   2K   77.23%   1m 23s

↑12.6%   ↑15.8%   ↑2.3%   ↓11.1%
vs last 7 days

Last 7 days ▼   AUDIENCE OVERVIEW ＞

Example: Facebook Page Demographics

What: 55% of fans are female.

So What: 70% of our customers are female. This gap is surprising.

Now What: We have to analyze our Facebook approach + content to determine why this is and if further action should be taken.

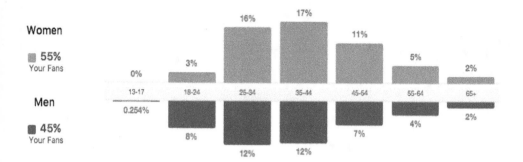

Women

■ 55%
Your Fans

Men

■ 45%
Your Fans

Power Tip:
It is also possible that some data doesn't contain insights or actions. Some data is just noise and can be a distraction from the metrics that matter. Consider which information is most meaningful for your business.

Analytics and Optimization

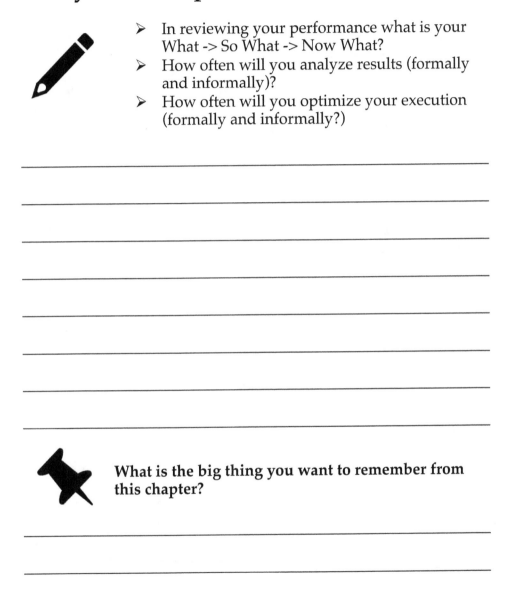

- ➢ In reviewing your performance what is your What -> So What -> Now What?
- ➢ How often will you analyze results (formally and informally)?
- ➢ How often will you optimize your execution (formally and informally?)

_____

_____

_____

_____

_____

_____

_____

What is the big thing you want to remember from this chapter?

_____

_____

Go to www.ThatActuallyWorks.com/DigitalMarketing for your free action planner and bonus resources.

Chapter 16: ROI

ROI stands for Return on Investment – it is one of the most talked about areas in measuring digital marketing but arguably calculating ROI is not one of the most important - and I worked in finance for many years!

Of course you need to be sure that your digital marketing efforts are generating a positive return, but calculating a specific ROI is usually incredibly difficult and also not very useful. The reason is because it's only really meaningful if you can compare it to other investments.

That being said, evaluating if you are getting a return on your investment is extremely important. Many businesses come up with a plan and execute without checking whether or not it is generating positive results for their business.

In this chapter we'll explore ROI – what it is, how to measure it, and how to know if your digital investment is paying out for your business.

Calculating ROI

ROI is calculated as: ROI = (Return – Investment)/Investment. Seems pretty straightforward right? There are only two things involved – the return and the investment.

The reality is that ROI is very difficult to calculate for any marketing activity. The reason for this is that we know that marketing is a process, and that people have multiple touchpoints with a business before they buy. Many marketing investments are challenging to calculate the return on. What is the ROI of a print ad? Or PR efforts? How many customers did you get from it?

It is difficult to answer these questions, and even if we create a marketing execution that drives action (like clicks) where we can measure, the risk is that we attribute the sale entirely to the last click. If this was true nobody would invest in brand building and 100% of marketing budgets would go to conversion tactics.

By now we know that marketing is a process, and multiple things contribute to an ultimate sale. Our goal in evaluating ROI is to make smart investment choices that grow our business.

Calculating the Return

The return is what you get out of your investment. While this seems straightforward it isn't. The reason we use KPIs in digital marketing is because tracing activities back to sales isn't easy.

Power Tip:
If you are calculating the return in your ROI, be sure that you consider the profit (not revenue) based on the lifetime value of a customer, which is usually more than just a single purchase. Many of the businesses that want to know the ROI of digital marketing don't actually know their customer lifetime profit.

Attribution modeling is an approach that has been developed for businesses to do a better job at distributing the "credit" for a sale across touchpoints. The idea of attribution modeling is to choose an approach to determine how different touchpoints contributed to a sale.

- Last click/first click attribution – This gives all of the credit of a sale to the last or first clicks before a purchase was made.
- Distributed attribution – There are a few models that can be used to distribute the credit of a sale across touchpoints.
- Even attribution - Every touchpoint gets even credit for contributing to a sale.
- Data-based attribution – This is where you conduct an in-depth analysis to understand how different touchpoints contribute to sales and attribute future sales based on the data model.

For most businesses that rely on multiple online and offline touchpoints, calculating the return from any one activity is a challenge. Longer sales cycle purchases are also difficult to measure.

Big Idea:
If your KPIs are set up well based on objectives and goals, they should be sufficient to justify your investment, even if they can't directly link to sales. This is why most businesses rely on KPIs instead of an ROI calculation.

Calculating the Investment

Calculating the investment is usually a little more straightforward, but it is important to include all of the costs.

As you consider your costs of a marketing activity, consider:
- Setup costs
- Launch costs

- Content costs
- Media or promotion costs
- Running costs
- Maintenance costs

Why Do We Need ROI?

ROI is difficult to measure (and we only touched the surface of the complexity here) and also isn't likely to be very accurate. Most businesses that are aggressive about calculating ROI for digital don't even calculate ROI for any other marketing investments.

So do we need ROI?

No. We don't need ROI as a calculation, but we do need to calculate if our investments are paying out. Many businesses don't calculate return or ROI on any investment. But with digital we do have lots of data, so we should calculate whether or not our money is well spent.

Analysis of marketing ROI should focus on answering three questions.

1) Is this investment paying out, meaning is it generating a positive return?
2) Is this investment better or worse than our other investments?
3) Could we be generating a better return on our investment?

Is the Investment Paying Out?

Rather than focusing on an ROI number, ask yourself if the investment is likely to be profit positive.

Backwards Math – What Would it Take?

The first calculation is backwards math, where you aim to answer the question what would it take for this to payout.

Contest Example
I'm creating a contest and want to understand what my goal should be to have a positive ROI. How many customers do I need to break even?

The contest is projected to:
- Reach 2,000 people
- Cost $200
- A new customer is about = $100 lifetime value

I would need two new customers to break even ($200/$100). This translates to a conversion rate of 0.1%. I now have a clear target in mind and based on historical executions I can determine whether or not this is reasonable to achieve.

To benchmark this cost I can also look at my cost per reach and compare it vs. other channels. Even though the quality of the impression may be different, it can be helpful to benchmark whether the cost per reach is comparable to other channels.
- Reach 2,000 people
- Cost $200
- Cost per reach of $0.10 to reach a new person

Social Media Management Example
I'm considering investing in social media management for my insurance agency. We get about 100 comments a month (positive and negative).
- Cost of management $2,000/month
- Lifetime profit value of customer $500
- Need 4 new customers a month to break even ($2,000/$500)

- 1 in every 25 commenters needs to be converted into a customer for this to payout
- Possibly also an impact from people who see the comments but aren't the commenter

Backwards math asks the question of what does this need to payout and it is a simple way to answer the question of whether or not an investment has positive ROI.

Comparing Investment Choices?

One of the goals of an ROI analysis is to allocate your budget better. In order to be able to do this you need similar comparisons of the value (and cost) of different marketing investments.

This is very challenging since all investments are different, and comparing impressions or leads for different channels isn't always accurate (since they are usually different quality) it can give you an idea of your investment result relative to other choices.

Contest Example
To benchmark this cost I can also look at my cost per reach and compare it vs. other channels. Even though the quality of the impression may be different, it can be helpful to benchmark whether the cost per reach is comparable to other channels.

- Reach 2,000 people
- Cost $200
- Cost per reach of $0.10 to reach a new person

I could also look at my cost per email address/lead acquisition. Not all leads are equal quality (and contests do tend to be lower) but it is another number I can use to evaluate my investment. I could compare this to other email acquisition costs.

- 50 entries in the contest
- Cost $200
- Cost of $4 per email address ($200/50)

Improving ROI

With many of our digital marketing efforts we know they are working, so the question isn't really if they have a positive ROI. If we believe we have a positive ROI our focus should shift to growing and improving our ROI.

Can you get better return with the same investment?

Can you get the same return with a lower investment?

- Investment:
    - Reduce time spent with tools and processes
    - Reuse and repurpose content
    - Determine what something is "worth" and set a budget

- Return:
    - Test and learn to improve over time
    - Analyze results to grow
    - Increase your reach since your investment in content is fixed

Big Idea:
In many instances you can generate better return on your time/effort investment by focusing on quick math and improving ROI. THINK IMPACT. Focus your measurement efforts where you can have the biggest impact on your results.

ROI and Value of Investment

➤ How can you calculate the return or benefit of your digital investment? Is ROI right or are there other methods?

➤ What action can you take to improve ROI and how do you operationalize this?

What is the big thing you want to remember from this chapter?

Go to www.ThatActuallyWorks.com/DigitalMarketing for your free action planner and bonus resources.

PART 4: GETTING STARTED

Now that we've covered all of the digital marketing tools you probably have many ideas of what you could do to grow your business.

Most businesses could use most digital marketing tools. The question is which tools are the most effective at driving impact for YOUR business.

At Boot Camp Digital our motto is THINK IMPACT. Whether it is personal productivity, business priorities, or digital marketing, the key to success is to focus where you can have the biggest impact.

Often businesses get excited about the potential of digital marketing and try to execute too many things too quickly. Success in digital requires excellence in execution.

Do fewer things better versus many things poorly.

Once you have mastered one channel add more to your strategy.

Chapter 17: Prioritizing Digital Marketing

With so many choices it can be difficult to know where to focus. With no end to what you **could** do you need to decide what you **should** do.

After reviewing all of the different digital marketing channels and tools, there's no doubt you have many ideas and are eager to get started. The key is to decide what to focus on to drive the biggest impact to your business.

There are no easy answers to how to prioritize, but there are two models that you can use to help prioritize your digital marketing spending.

Each business is different in their resources, current digital execution, and growth aspirations, so they will all prioritize differently.

Prioritization: Hero, Hub, Hygiene

The first method that can be used to prioritize your spending is Hero, Hub, Hygiene. This model is adapted from the Google content model.

Consider the digital marketing activities you are thinking of executing and categorize them as Hero, Hub, or Hygiene. Different businesses may place different activities under each category – it depends on the size of your business, your customer expectations, and your digital maturity.

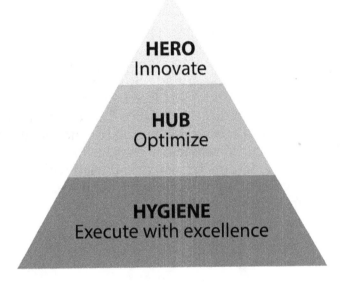

Hygiene

What it is:
Hygiene activities are those that you have to do as a respected business. From a non-digital standpoint this would be things like have a phone line, execute customer service, have business cards, etc.

How much effort:
For established businesses hygiene should take up about 20% of your digital marketing efforts. Less established businesses may spend more time and effort.

How to approach it:
Your goal with hygiene activities should be to complete them as efficiently as possible with good execution. It can't be awful or embarrassing for your business, but it also doesn't need to be the best or most expensive execution. For example, if you sell a beauty product at retailers you need a website. You don't need the best website, but you need a good website that looks professional and represents your business well.

Big Idea:
We sometimes avoid or ignore hygiene for a variety of reasons. I had a friend with an outdated, terrible website for his business that he just couldn't seem to get around to updating. From the outside it was clearly the #1 thing preventing his success, but he was so focused on other things he just never got around to it. This framework, if used well, can help you see blind spots in your hygiene areas that could be limiting your success.

Hub

What it is:
Hub activities are proven strategies that will grow your business. These are the things that you know work, or they typically work for your industry or business. These are the digital marketing activities that really drive your business forward. This is the area that generates the most ROI for your business. By continuing to improve and optimize proven strategies, your business will grow over time.

How much effort:
For established businesses hub activities should represent 60% - 70% of your marketing efforts. Many businesses have a tendency to move on after implementing something. Once it is running they move to the next. Instead, stay focused on growing your results to

maximize your ROI.

How to approach it:
The goal of Hub activities is to optimize and improve your execution and results. For example, if you are already running Facebook ads and getting results, spending time optimizing and improving your ads will grow your return on investment. The focus here is improvement. In a rapidly evolving digital space, businesses must continue to invest in proven working strategies to continue their success.

Hero

What it is:
Hero activities are your innovation activities. They are the new things that aren't yet proven. These could be different for every business. For example, LinkedIn ads are well established, but if my business hasn't used them yet, these would be a Hero activity.

How much effort:
Hero innovation content should take up 10% - 20% of your efforts, depending on your digital maturity. Since innovations usually don't have well-established best practices and you don't have experience with them yet they often take more investment to setup and get running. It is important to remember that your return isn't guaranteed with Hero activities, so you want to limit your investment, as there is a better chance that they fail than succeed.

How to approach it:
The goal of Hero activities is to move them into the hub. This means clear KPIs and targets with the ability to experiment and test to determine what works. The objective is to test and learn and establish what works so that a Hero activity can either be stopped or moved into the Hub.

Big Idea:
By categorizing activities as Hero, Hub, or Hygiene you can understand why you need to do an activity and also approach it correctly to maximize your return on investment.

Prioritization: Investment/Impact

While your hygiene activities may be a given, you will likely have more Hub and Hero activities than resources available. The next tool at your disposal to support prioritization is Investment Impact.

The idea is to plot your activities on the Investment/Impact chart below to determine which activities are most likely to bring you the results you want.

It may be difficult to know for sure the investment of an activity, but do your best to estimate and be sure to consider all of the costs (run costs, promotion costs, technical issues, etc.).

The impact may also not be exactly known, but you can start with rough estimates or do some "back of the envelope math" to consider how many people could be reached or converted by your efforts.

Even if you don't have the exact investment or impact, graphing your activities in this way (especially if you are tough and honest) will bring clarity to your choices and help you decide where to focus.

Example:
At Boot Camp Digital we use this framework to graph and prioritize all of our marketing activities. When looking at it in this way we often find that we misallocate our efforts by focusing on things that don't have a big impact on our business. THINK IMPACT is our corporate slogan ;-)

Graph all of your activities based on Investment/Impact and you'll find they fall into one of four quadrants.

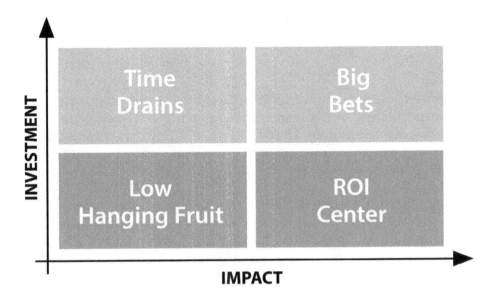

IMPACT

Big Idea:
Be sure that you include **all of the costs** involved in executing. This includes setup costs, launch costs, promotion or media costs, running costs, and optimization costs.

Low Hanging Fruit

Low hanging fruit are areas that are low investment but also low impact. These are things that aren't incredibly impactful but are easy to do. For example, these could be things like updating social media cover images. This section often is made up of odds and ends.

Since items in this section aren't high impact they should be executed as efficiently as possible. For example, I don't want to spend thousands of dollars and countless hours to create the best cover image ever (after all – it is low impact) but I want a good cover image. Efficiency over excellence since the impact is low.

ROI Center

The next section is the ROI Center – this is the section that will drive your ROI and where you want to execute with excellence because the results matter. The ROI Center is low investment but high impact. These are the things that can really move your business forward without too much investment.

The goal with ROI Center activities should be to execute with excellence. These activities have the ability to grow your business and are high impact – so you need to execute well to drive impact.

Big Bets

A big bet is something that has a big investment but also a big impact. This is something that is expensive and maybe difficult to execute well, but the payout could be big. The challenge with big bets is to be sure that you have correctly estimated the impact so that they aren't actually time drains.

Big bets usually require investment of time, money, and effort to execute with excellence and make them work well. Be sure that you have sufficient resources to allocate to your big bets so you don't end up poorly executing something that doesn't drive results for your business.

Time Drains

These are the worst activities to do! High investment but low impact. No business would deliberately work on time drains, but they often arise from an idea that seems like a good idea but it is actually small in scope and impact when you really think about it. For example, a suggestion for a new niche product for my business is very expensive (high investment) but the impact is probably small since it targets a niche.

Time drains should never be invested in, but most businesses miss them because they "seem like good ideas." Run some basic numbers to estimate the real impact.

You may also find that activities that seemed like they were in other quadrants became time drains. Be aware of activities that are growing in scope or investment, or are smaller impact than you thought. Don't be afraid to rebalance.

Big Idea:
Reassess your activities and priorities regularly, as you may initially over or under-estimate. Check that low hanging fruit doesn't turn into a time drain because you hit a snag or had a technical issue, and know how much time, money, and effort you are willing to invest.

The Investment/Impact Framework, if used correctly, can be extremely impactful in helping you prioritize your business. This activity is best done as a team and you need to be tough to know where activities really lie. Often times you'll find that your pet projects or "great ideas" are actually a time drain.

Remember:
Do fewer things better vs. taking on too much. Excellent execution is required for success and if you spread your efforts too thin you may find that you don't execute anything well enough to get results.

Prioritizing Digital Marketing

➤ How do your marketing plans break out between Hero, Hub and Hygiene?

➤ How do your ideas rank on the investment/impact grid? Do you have the right balance to grow your business?

_____

_____

_____

_____

_____

_____

_____

What is the big thing you want to remember from this chapter?

_____

_____

Go to www.ThatActuallyWorks.com/DigitalMarketing for your free action planner and bonus resources.

Chapter 18: Building Your Digital Marketing Plan

The ball is now in your court. It is time to take action and drive impact to grow your business.

Determine Your Resources

As you begin to move forward in your execution determine the resources that you have (both time and money) to execute. Many things take more time and effort than you realize. Once you execute something you still need to have capacity to analyze and optimize to grow your results.

Determine the resources that you have available as you decide how much to take on.

Insource vs. Outsource

Even if you plan to outsource, investing in this book is a first step in the right direction. If you don't know something well enough, you won't be able to manage your agency and hold them accountable.

From a trend standpoint, more and more large organizations are insourcing the majority of their digital marketing efforts. They still use agencies for some aspects, but they have internal experts and are managing more and more internally.

When determining if you should insource or outsource consider the following:

- How technical or specialized is the skill needed to execute? *The less specialized the easier to execute internally.*

- Do you have the capability internally? *Consider if there are adequate resources to execute well.*

- What is the cost for an agency to execute? *Agencies are usually more expensive, but also have the expertise.*

If your goal is DIY or insource, start small, master one thing and then move on to the next.

 Remember:
Even if you outsource you still need some time to onboard your agency, set expectations, and execute with excellence. Don't take on too much at once.

Build Your Digital Marketing Plan

To initiate your digital marketing efforts, build a clear and time-oriented execution plan. Once you've decided which activities to take on, build out your action plan.

It is usually helpful to time your action plan into four buckets based on:
- Immediate
- 3 Months
- 6 – 9 Months
- Next year

Once an activity is on the horizon create more specific steps to execute so you are clear on what needs to happen when to get results. It is helpful to break down the steps so that you can be realistic about what is involved in the execution. Sometimes tasks that seem quick are actually more challenging, which can be uncovered by mapping out the steps.

Action:
If you've been completing the action planner through this book you should be ready to go and clear on your priorities. If you have not downloaded it yet you can find it at **www.ThatActuallyWorksBooks.com/DigitalMarketing.**

Pro Tips to Get Started

Some of these have been mentioned in the book, but keep them in mind to maximize your results.

1) Start with strategy. Know WHY you are doing something before you get started. Every aspect of your execution should build towards your strategy.
2) Set KPIs. A KPI is what you want to achieve from your efforts and how you will track your success. It is important to stay focused and grow impact.
3) Do fewer things better. Master something before you move on to the next.
4) Be realistic about investments. Some things take more time and effort than expected, and you may hit technical issues.
5) The devil is in the details. Some details can make or break your success – make sure you nail the details that matter.
6) Great content is vital. Invest in excellent content to break-through the clutter and get noticed in a more competitive landscape.
7) Test, test, test. If you aren't getting results or if the success of something really matters invest in testing to maximize your results.

8) Make time for analytics. Many businesses just execute, execute, execute. They don't step back to check that their efforts are working before they continue to invest.

9) Prioritize your efforts. We often focus on the wrong things and miss the things that matter most. *This is something I regularly kick myself for.*

10) Think Impact. In everything you do. Think Impact and focus on what matters most.

Building Your Digital Marketing Plan

➢ What resources do you have to execute digital marketing initiatives?
➢ What will you insource vs. outsource?
➢ What will you do when – immediately, medium-term and long-term?

_____

_____

_____

_____

_____

_____

_____

What is the big thing you want to remember from this chapter?

_____

_____

Go to www.ThatActuallyWorks.com/DigitalMarketing for your free action planner and bonus resources

BOOT★CAMP
DIGITAL

Want to take your social media and digital marketing skills to the next level? Go to **www.BootCampDigital.com** to see how we can help you succeed.

What We Offer at Boot Camp Digital:

- Online training courses from Beginner to Advanced
- Industry-recognized Certifications in Social Media, Digital Marketing, Content, SEO and more
- Live workshops around the U.S.
- Customized corporate team training
- Digital Marketing and Social Media consulting
- 1:1 Coaching and Strategic Planning

Connect with Us Online

 bootcampdigital
 @bootcampdigital

 @bootcampdigital
 Boot Camp Digital

Contact us for speaking, training, consulting, seminar or workshop opportunities at: info@bootcampdigital.com or call us at **513-223-3878**.

About the Author

Krista Neher is the CEO of Boot Camp Digital, a bestselling author, an international speaker and a seasoned marketing executive.

She has worked with leading companies like Google, P&G, General Mills, Nike, GE, The United States Senate, Prudential, Remax and more. She has been a featured expert in the Wall Street Journal, New York Times, CNN, Associated Press, Wired Magazine and more. Krista is passionate about social media and created one of the first accredited social media certification programs in the world.

Connect with Krista Online

   Krista.Neher.Pro

   @KristaNeher

@KristaNeher

   Krista Neher

Want to Work with Krista?

Krista works with a wide variety of businesses across industries and can work with you in a number of ways:

- Keynote presentations
- Workshops
- Breakout sessions
- Customized internal training programs
- 1:1 Coaching
- Executive training
- Corporate training
- Consulting
- Strategic planning

Contact Krista for speaking, training, consulting, seminar or workshops: info@bootcampdigital.com or **513-223-3878**

CPSIA information can be obtained
at www.ICGtesting.com
Printed in the USA
FSHW021732301221
87304FS